PSYCHIATRY

Cavendish
Publishing
Limited

London • Sydney

PSYCHIATRY

Joan Gomez, MBBS, FRCPsych, DPM, DHMSA

SERIES EDITOR
Dr Walter Scott, LLB (Hons),
MBBS, MRCGP, DObstRCOG

Cavendish
Publishing
Limited

London • Sydney

First published in Great Britain 1997 by Cavendish Publishing Limited, The Glass House, Wharton Street, London WC1X 9PX.

Telephone: 0171-278 8000 Facsimile: 0171-278 8080

E-mail: info@cavendishpublishing.com

Visit our Home Page on http://www.cavendishpublishing.com

Gomez, Joan
Psychiatry – (Medico-legal practioner series)
1. Psychiatry
I. Title II. Scott, Walter
616.8'9'0024344

ISBN 1 85941 017 0

Printed and bound in Great Britain by
Biddles Ltd, Guildford and King's Lynn

FOREWORD

Those who have shown an interest in the 'medico-legal practitioner's series' may like to learn something about its origins and the history of its development. With this objective in mind I will devote a few moments to the past and I will then turn to the future which is, after all, even more important for us.

I first conceived the idea of such a theme in the Summer of 1994. By that stage I had been preparing reports for lawyers on cases of alleged medical negligence for about five years. I had also been looking at other doctors' reports for the same length of time and it was becoming increasingly apparent to me that one of the lawyers' most difficult tasks was to understand the medical principles clearly. To be fair to the lawyers, there were some doctors who did not always make matters very clear. This, coupled with the difficulty which many doctors have in understanding the legal concept of negligence and related topics, merely served to compound the problem.

It therefore occurred to me that a possible solution to the difficulty would be to develop some material on medical topics written by doctors who had a particular interest in the medico-legal field. The authors would require at least four attributes. First, they would have to be specialists in their own field. Secondly, they would need the ability to explain their subject to non-medical readers in clear language that was easy to follow. Put another way there was no case for writing a medical textbook for their students or colleagues. Thirdly, they would require a fair amount of experience in medico-legal reporting, analysis of cases and dealing with lawyers who were defending or advancing cases. This would give them an understanding of how the lawyer's mind works and an appreciation of the medical areas which can cause difficulty in practice and where accidents can happen. There would be a contrast with medical books where the emphasis is on the diseases which most commonly present to the doctor. Fourthly, the authors would need the ability to work in harmony with a series editor who was anxious to achieve some degree of uniformity across the whole range of the material.

Having identified these four points as being desirable characteristics of the potential authors the next step was to find a publisher who would be sufficiently interested to give the project the support it needed. This was to be no small task and was likely to involve a very long-term commitment because, after the initial launch, it was inevitable that much more work would be required by way of future editions and additional titles. I was most fortunate to be dealing with Cavendish Publishing in connection with my own book, *The General Practitioner and the Law of Negligence,* and I am pleased to say that they seized this new idea with the utmost enthusiasm. At last I thought that the 'medico-legal practitioner series' would become a reality.

It then only remained to find the authors, commission the work and wait for the results. It was at this point, however, that I began to realise that I was still only at the very beginning of my task. Eventually, however, after numerous discussions with various people a team materialised. When the early chapters of the first books began to arrive it was starting to look as though we really were going to have something which was quite unique. When the final manuscripts arrived my confidence increased still further. More than two years after my initial plans the first set of books has become available and the dream has turned into reality.

This, then, is how the project came into being but it must be emphasised that, in a manner of speaking, we have really only just got ourselves started. For the series to thrive it must be flexible and respond to the needs of its users. It must adapt to medical developments and legal changes. Clinical subjects are a primary consideration but it is my firm intention to expand the series to involve other areas of interest. Indeed the first non-clinical title should appear almost as soon as the initial set becomes available. On a more long term basis, I would like the series to cover every field of expertise that is of concern to the medico-legal practitioner.

Uniformity of approach and clarity of presentation must be hallmarks of the individual titles but the series as a whole must be independent and objective. If we can aspire to these criteria we should achieve a fair measure of success in assisting our readers to give good advice to their clients.

It remains for me to express my gratitude to all the authors and to the publishers for their cooperation. In another kind of way I will be equally grateful to all our readers for placing their reliance on us and for sharing our optimism.

Walter Scott
Series Editor
Slough
August 1996

ACKNOWLEDGMENT

I am grateful to Dr Walter Scott for all his help and encouragement.

CONTENTS

CHAPTER ONE

HOW PSYCHIATRY AND THE LAW MEET

Psychiatry is more intimately involved with the law than any other medical specialty. There is no Gynaecological Health Act nor Orthopaedic Review Tribunal to match those for mental health. Only the psychiatrist is empowered to deprive a patient of his freedom, albeit under strict legal conditions. Most important of all, psychiatry has an input in all other areas of medicine. Examples are the emotional impact of a diagnosis of cancer, or the psychological reaction to a hysterectomy or a heart attack. The severity of such reactions ranges from the trivial to the crippling.

This chapter outlines the main areas where psychiatrists and lawyers interact, from medical negligence to mitigation of an offence. They include:

1   Medical negligence
    • by other medical practitioners;
    • by psychiatrists.
2   Compensation for other injuries (eg at work, traffic accidents etc)
    • physical injury with psychological disturbance;
    • psychiatric symptoms after head injury;
    • post-concussional syndrome;
    • psychological trauma and psychiatric damage.
3   Legal issues in ordinary psychiatric practice
4   Testamentary capacity
5   Competence to manage money and affairs
    • receivership and The Court of Protection.
6   Marriage and other contracts
7   Mentally abnormal offenders
    • fitness to stand trial;
    • fitness to plead;
    • not guilty by reason of insanity;
    • diminished responsibility;
    • automatism;
    • infanticide;
    • amnesia;
    • drugs and alcohol;
    • mutism;

- confessions, false and true.

8 Victims of torture

- applications for asylum.

9 Fitness to drive

MEDICAL NEGLIGENCE

For medico-legal practitioners, medical negligence is a growth industry. Many firms of solicitors now have a department devoted to such cases. The typical scenario is of a medical or surgical procedure which goes wrong, often from the cumulative effect of a series of trivial errors, or a misdiagnosis. No matter what the alleged physical damage, a claim for psychological suffering or psychiatric harm is commonly put forward. Psychiatric reports are then required by both plaintiff's and defendant's solicitors.

The issues to focus on:

1 Does the plaintiff have a defined psychiatric disorder?

2 If so, to what extent has it been caused by the medical incident complained of?

The psychiatric report should be based not only on an interview and psychiatric examination, but on careful perusal of the medical notes, any reports already made, and, often most revealing of all, the GP records. If these are studied before seeing the patient, the psychiatrist's questions can be more pertinent. For example, if the patient complains of depression, the records may show that he has suffered from previous episodes before the present medical involvement. On the other hand, the patient may have consulted the GP several times during the period in which he claims to have been 'terribly depressed' yet there is no record to show this.

The psychiatrist's assessment takes precedence over others on psychiatric matters, although the lay public, lawyers and other doctors all tend to feel that they have special expertise in this area.

Case

At the age of 25 JP had five children. When her youngest was four months old, she found herself pregnant again and asked for a termination and sterilisation. The termination was carried out without complication but JP's obesity made the placing of the Hulka clips on the tubes, for sterilisation, difficult. A year later, JP became pregnant. The consultant carried out a suction termination and sterilisation, but the wound became infected. This caused JP considerable abdominal pain, which was slow to clear up and involved administering a variety of antibiotics. Intercourse was painful, and, anyway, JP felt no faith in the sterilisation. She 'went right off sex' and her husband became frustrated and impatient. Five years later she claimed still to be suffering from depression and loss of libido. Psychiatric examination revealed no symptoms of depression, but JP was full of resentment towards hospital doctors and males in general. She had separated from her husband after numerous rows over marital relations, and she claimed that he had forced intercourse on her when she was still sore. It was argued that JP's ongoing distaste for sex and anger towards men was due, at least in part, to the insensitive behaviour of her partner.

Psychiatric negligence

Psychiatrists are sued more often by people other than their patients. The Schizophrenia Fellowship has collected 17 recent cases involving paranoid schizophrenics who had attacked other people under the influence of their delusions. The psychiatrists were blamed for releasing these patients or not arranging effective supervision, when they should have known that they were putting others at risk.

Christopher Clunies was one such patient. He killed a complete stranger, Mr Zito, who was standing near him on a railway platform. His wife has begun a campaign.

Trevor Holland, a known paedophile under psychiatric care, escaped while on a therapeutic outing to Chessington Zoo, a popular venue for children. The family of a former victim, who had received threatening letters from Holland, were terrified and blamed the psychiatrist for his escape. Fortunately, the man was recaptured before any harm had resulted.

If a psychiatric patient commits suicide, the relatives may claim that the psychiatrist had neglected his duty of care.

Cases brought by patients themselves against their psychiatrists often involve their treatment. Electroconvulsive therapy (ECT) is sometimes blamed years later for a patient's memory problems; or the side-effects of neuroleptic medication, especially the movement disorder, tardive dyskinesia, maybe the subject of complaint. ECT has been condemned, but may have been life-saving to an acutely suicidal patient, while neuroleptics have been the major treatment for serious psychoses for four decades. It was largely due to their introduction in 1953 that indefinite incarceration, of schizophrenic patients in particular, is now seldom necessary and huge mental hospitals are being closed. An adverse result of these closures is the acute shortage of psychiatric beds, so that there is pressure on psychiatrists to discharge their patients as soon as possible.

A particular difficulty for psychiatrists is that, due to the nature of their work, a patient who brings a case may have a paranoid psychosis, or an obsessional neurosis with paranoid ideas, and may develop into a vexatious litigant before the illness is obvious.

Another important reason for a psychiatrist or his hospital or health authority becoming involved in litigation is when the doctor's judgment is challenged in cases detained under the Mental Health Act 1987. This is not a problem of negligence and is dealt with in Chapter 12.

COMPENSATION FOR OTHER INJURIES

Aside from medical negligence, the main areas for claiming compensation for personal injury, including psychological effects, include:

1 Injuries at work or school.
2 Accidents involving other parties, especially road traffic accidents.
3 Faulty goods or equipment.

The psychological consequences of an injury depend crucially on the circumstances:

- the sex, age and occupation of the injured party;
- the site of the injury;
- elements in the person's social background, for instance dependent relatives;
- scarring and disfigurement;
- loss of function, including for pleasurable activities.

Case

At the time of his accident RB was working as a props man at a major provincial theatre. He was 32, married with two young children and a mortgage. He was working on a new set with a mockup balcony on the front (only) of a house when the structure collapsed, pitching RB some eight feet onto the stage. There was some doubt about whether he lost consciousness, but none about the incapacitating back pain he developed. There was no bone injury.

Because of his pain, which did not abate despite drugs and physiotherapy and a range of expensive alternative therapies, RB could no longer play squash, at which he had excelled, nor even enjoy active games with his sons. He could not cope with his work, which involved bending and lifting, nor do DIY at home. He was a miserable companion, began drinking heavily and marital relations suffered as a result.

The orthopaedic specialists made their differing assessments, and the psychiatrists, too, had difficulties in coming to a conclusion. To what extent were RB's low mood, alcohol use and protracted back pain due to the fall? It emerged that he had considerable gambling debts and the fall had come after RB had been drinking. Was he clinically depressed? The settlement was a compromise.

RB's case is a common example of one of the ways in which psychological injury can attract compensation. Others include:

- psychiatric symptoms after head injury, including the post-concussional syndrome;
- psychological trauma with psychiatric damage.

Psychiatric symptoms after head injury

Head injury is common, particularly in traffic accidents, with a peak incidence in men between 16 and 24 years of age, where alcohol is often found to be a factor.

Psychiatric *sequelae* come in two packs:

1 A minority with serious and lasting cognitive deficits, such as a persistent defect of memory.
2 A large majority with emotional symptoms and sometimes a personality change which may lead to long-lasting disability.

Acute effects: all but the mildest cases lose consciousness at the time of the injury, followed by two kinds of memory loss:

- retrograde amnesia: for the period immediately before the incident;
- anterograde or post-traumatic amnesia: the longer the period involved the worse the prognosis.

Difficulty with memory and calculation may persist in serious cases, with a generalised intellectual deterioration, personality change towards a coarsening of behaviour, loss of drive and irritability merging into aggressiveness. Left-sided parietal and temporal injuries are especially associated with cognitive defects, while frontal lobe damage affects the personality.

Case

CH, aged 36, a Pakistani businessman, was caught in a collision on the M25. He received severe head injuries which resulted in gross memory and personality changes. From a pleasant, friendly family man he became aggressive and unmanageable, demanding meals, sex and the return of his car in an insightless, uninhibited way. He could only be contained in a secure ward.

Since CH had not been at fault he was awarded substantial compensation on the strength of the psychiatric report. The sum, the quantum for damages, involved assessment of loss of earnings, physical inconvenience, social discredit, mental distress and loss of the society of his wife and children. The psychiatrist was expected to give an opinion on the extent to which CH's injuries were responsible for his situation. This was based on his full life history to date, his current mental state and a neurological opinion, including appropriate scans. Psychometric testing by a psychologist might be helpful in such cases.

Much more frequent, and often equivocal, are cases of head injury that do not involve serious brain damage. Their long-term sequelae cover a range of possible symptoms:

- personality change, irritability;
- headaches, dizziness, fatigue, poor concentration;
- neurotic disorders, such as phobias, depression;
- schizophrenia-like syndromes with delusions;
- poor memory;
- epileptic phenomena.

Older patients fare the worst.

Rehabilitation is time-consuming, with disruption of work and social life, and is often only partially successful.

Post-concussional syndrome

This comprises a group of symptoms which occur as a result of a closed head injury severe enough to cause loss of consciousness and sometimes the onset of fits. Typical symptoms are:

- poor concentration;
- poor memory;
- headaches, dizziness;
- labile mood;
- reduced tolerance of alcohol;
- visual disturbances;
- depression or anxiety;
- exhaustion.

(See Jacobson, RR (1995) and Lishman (1987) in the section on Further Reading, p 127.)

Headaches and dizziness may persist for some months, but in only 1% are they present after a year, usually with no neurological abnormality. Although the original insult was organic, psychological factors, depending on the patient's circumstances, are likely to prolong the symptoms.

Case

DF was involved in a car accident the day after he was made redundant. His minor head injury led to a plethora of symptoms which covered his jobless state and held some promise of financial aid. He was not malingering, but his injury did not account for his many symptoms.

Psychological trauma and psychiatric damage

Psychological trauma is often a concomitant of physical injury, but not always. A psychological shock, or 'nervous shock' as some lawyers term it, may be a threat to personal safety or a sudden loss, including the death of another person. It may cause psychological damage. A normal emotional reaction, including an adjustment reaction or an acute stress reaction, does not rate as a basis for compensation.

What is valid includes:

- lasting personality change, perhaps with anti-social behaviour;
- clinical depression;
- prolonged anxiety state, perhaps with panics or phobia;
- post-traumatic stress disorder (PTSD);
- psychosis: rarely precipitated by psychological trauma;
- taking to drink or drugs in some circumstances;
- pathological grief: intense symptoms lasting more than six months.

Bereavement: sadness and distress are normal and do not qualify for compensation. If a psychiatric disorder, usually clinical anxiety or depression, but exceptionally post-traumatic stress disorder, results from a sudden, dramatic loss there may be a case. The Hillsborough disaster broke new ground when the trauma of seeing the event on television sharpened the horror of the bereavement and was judged to be equivalent to being present at the catastrophe.

LEGAL ISSUES IN ORDINARY PSYCHIATRIC PRACTICE

The same issues apply as in other medical practice.

Confidentiality: extra sensitive in psychiatry when sexual matters are discussed as routine. Confidentiality can be broken if there is judged to be a risk to the patient or another person, or to prevent the commission of a crime. Risk to the patient or another is more likely in psychiatric patients than those with medical conditions, obviously.

Consent to treatment: a competent adult has the right to refuse medical treatment even if this involves his death or disablement. For most forms of treatment it is sufficient to explain its nature and the probable side-effects.

Informed consent, for instance when taking part in a clinical trial, requires detailed discussion of all possible side-effects.

Consent to treatment is not required if:

- the patient is unconscious but a reasonable person would consent to the treatment;
- death or grave harm is likely to result if treatment is not given and there is doubt about the patient's competence;
- it is an emergency and treatment is needed to prevent immediate serious harm to the patient or to someone else, or to prevent a serious crime.

Points to consider:

- does the patient have the mental capacity to understand and refuse treatment?
- has the patient been coerced into refusal by other people? (Jehovah's Witnesses, other religious groups).

Competence issues arise in cases of mental retardation, children and those with mental illness. Can the patient understand and retain the information he is given about the treatment, does he believe it, and is he able to use it to make an informed choice? A paranoid patient may believe the psychiatrist is out to kill him.

Compulsory treatment in psychiatric case: The Mental Health Act 1987 does not allow for compulsory treatment for physical conditions, but does so in some cases of mental illness.

Compulsory admission to hospital and treatment: there are legal provisions for patients who are a danger to themselves or to others because of mental disorder and refuse to accept the treatment they need. They have little or no insight into their illness. Various sections of the Mental Health Act are called into play:

Section 2: admission for assessment and if necessary, treatment. It runs for 28 days. Application must be made by the patient's nearest relative or an Approved Social Worker, backed up by recommendations from two doctors of whom one must be 'approved' as having special expertise in mental health.

Section 4: emergency admission for assessment, lasting 72 hours. Application is made by an Approved Social Worker, with a recommendation from one doctor who need not be on the approved list.

Case

A manic patient arrived at Buckingham Palace demanding entry and immediate coronation as King George VII. The police brought him to hospital where he was seen by a social worker and a doctor and admitted.

> *Section 3*: admission for treatment. It runs for six months and is then renewable. This can only be applied to patients with serious mental illness, severe mental impairment, or psychopathic disorder or (less severe) mental impairment when treatment is likely to have some beneficial effect and it is necessary for the health or safety of the patient or other person that he should receive this treatment.

The application and medical recommendations required are the same as for Section 2, but with greater detail from the doctors.

TESTAMENTARY CAPACITY

Disputes about the provisions of a will naturally arise after the death of the person concerned. If a close relative has been omitted or someone who had only known the testator for a comparatively short time benefits greatly, the testamentary capacity of the dead person may be in question. The notorious Dr Bodkin Adam of Eastbourne aroused suspicion because so many of his elderly patients favoured him in their wills, to the detriment of those who might reasonably have expected to inherit.

Any doctor who has been involved with the deceased – and a psychiatrist's view would carry the most weight – may be called upon to give an opinion about testamentary capacity. In cases of dementia in particular, where there is doubt in the solicitor's mind at the time of drawing up the will, a psychiatrist may be asked to examine the patient.

For the will to be valid the testator must be judged to be 'of sound disposing mind'. This requires:

- the ability to understand what a will is and its consequences;
- the subject's ability to remember what property he or she has, although not necessarily every detail;
- the ability to recall the names of all close relatives or others who might reasonably be expected to have a claim on the person's bounty. These could include a common law partner or some other person with a long association with the subject;
- the absence of an abnormal state of mind which might distort feelings or judgment relevant to making a will. A patient with delusions may still be able to make a valid will, provided these do not impinge on the process of making a will. For example, a woman of 67, a chronic paranoid

schizophrenic, had a fixed delusion that her next door neighbour was tunnelling under her house to spy on her. Her relations with other people were unaffected and she made a will perfectly in keeping with what would have been expected.

Case

SP's situation was more complex. He had married three times and had five children from those marriages, with whom he had a good relationship, although his present wife did not get on with any of them. She had married him two years before his brief and final illness at the age of 71. He had lung cancer with secondaries in his brain. When he was in hospital he altered his will to leave everything to his wife. The solicitor was worried. After SP's death the matter went to court. The psychiatrist's report indicated that SP could hardly remember who anyone was: he had even tried to get into bed with another patient, believing that he was at home and she was his wife. The will was overturned.

COMPETENCE TO MANAGE MONEY AND AFFAIRS

If a patient, either in hospital or in the community, is incapable of managing his or her affairs, either temporarily or long term, because of mental disorder, arrangements must be made to protect his property and finances. The simplest and quickest method is for the patient to sign a Power of Attorney authorising someone else to act for him. At the time of signing the patient must be able to understand what he is doing. In early dementia and other situations in which the patient's mental capacity is likely to decline, an Enduring Power of Attorney can be arranged while he is still mentally fit enough.

Receivership is a more formal procedure, in which application is made to the Court of Protection to manage the patient's affairs. If the relatives are unwilling, it is the psychiatrist's duty to make the application. The charges made by the Court of Protection are quite heavy, so it is suitable only where there are substantial assets.

MARRIAGE AND OTHER CONTRACTS

If a person is suffering from mental impairment or a mental disorder such that he cannot understand what a contract is, it is considered void. In the case of marriage the union is annulled. Obviously these matters require psychiatric assessment.

Divorce: if one partner was apparently fit at the time of the marriage, but is later diagnosed as being 'of incurably unsound mind' this may be grounds for a divorce. Divorce law has been simplified over the years, but a psychiatric opinion is still required if one party claims to have been made psychiatrically ill by the behaviour of the other.

Related areas of civil law in which the psychiatrist may be involved are care proceedings with children and decisions about custody and adoption.

MENTALLY ABNORMAL OFFENDERS

Definitions

It is essential in criminal cases to use the terms referring to mental disorders precisely as they are defined in the Homicide Act 1957, and the Mental Health Act 1983.

1 *Mental abnormality*

Covers mental illness, all mental impairment and psychopathic disorder.

2 *Mental disorder*

Includes four areas:

- *Mental illness*: this encompasses the psychoses, neuroses and organic states as assessed clinically;
- *Arrested or incomplete development of mind*: this is subdivided into:
  - (i) *Severe mental impairment*: this includes severe impairment of intelligence and social functioning, with abnormally aggressive or seriously irresponsible conduct. The IQ is usually below 50,
  - (ii) *Mental impairment*: this involves significant impairment of intelligence and social functioning and abnormally aggressive or seriously irresponsible conduct, but not amounting to severe mental impairment. The IQ is likely to be between 50 and 70, although these levels are not included in the official definition;
- *Psychopathic disorder*: for legal purposes this is 'a persistent disorder or disability of mind' (whether or not including significant impairment of intelligence) which results in abnormally aggressive or seriously irresponsible conduct. Promiscuity or other immorality, sexual deviance, or dependence on drugs or alcohol do not, on their own, amount to mental disorder;
- *Any other disorder or disability of mind*: this includes some neuroses, personality disorders, drug or alcohol dependency, children's behaviour disorders, some learning disability and the aftermath of injury or illness. Unlike those above, these disorders cannot be taken as

a basis for detaining the patient in hospital under the Mental Health Act. They may, however, be considered in mitigation of an offence.

MENTAL ABNORMALITY AS A DEFENCE

Children, although not mentally abnormal, are among those who may not be considered responsible for their criminal acts. Those under 10 are generally exempt, while with those between the ages of 10–13 the prosecution must prove that the child knew that what he was doing was wrong. The Bulger case, in which two young boys murdered a two year old, cast doubt upon the innocence of children and provoked a reappraisal.

Not fit to stand trial: a severely mentally ill person, likely to be suffering from acute schizophrenia, mania or dementia, or profoundly subnormal, may be judged unfit to go to court. A hospital order may be made in his absence.

Not fit to plead: it is considered inhumane to put someone through a trial if, because of mental disability, he is unable to defend himself in court. To be fit to plead, the accused must be able to:

1 plead to the indictment: that is, understand the charge and the significance of pleading 'guilty' or 'not guilty';
2 comprehend the course of the proceedings of the trial, so as to make a sensible defence;
3 know that he might challenge a juror;
4 comprehend the details of the evidence. He must be able to instruct his lawyer. To 'prove' disability, two psychiatrists, of whom one must be on the 'approved' list, give reports before a jury. If it is decided that the accused is under disability his case is heard under the Criminal Procedure (Insanity and Unfitness to Plead) Act 1991. In a case of murder he may be sent to hospital indefinitely.

Not guilty by reason of insanity: since the introduction in 1957 of the concept of diminished responsibility, applied to killing another person, the defence of insanity is seldom used. It is embodied in the McNaghten Rules, laid down in 1843. Daniel McNaghten, a long-term paranoid schizophrenic, focused his delusions on the Conservative Party and decided to kill the Prime Minister. In error he shot the Prime Minister's secretary. To public outrage, he was found not guilty by reason of insanity. The rules laid down by the judges state that: 'it must be clearly proved that at the time of committing the act the accused was labouring under such a defect of reason, from disease of the mind, as not to know the nature and quality of the act he was doing, or, if he did know, that he did not know that what he was doing was wrong.'

These rules are still valid, but most cases are not clear cut and are better dealt with under the concept of diminished responsibility brought in by the

Homicide Act 1957. For instance this has replaced the Infanticide Act 1938: a mother who kills her baby may be assessed as in a disturbed state of mind due to giving birth or lactating, and thus less culpable.

Case

In 1996 Nicola Jordan, aged 20, suffocated her eight week old daughter and was found guilty of manslaughter, rather than murder. She was also convicted of causing grievous bodily harm to two other infants she had been looking after.

Cases like that of Sarah Thornton, who killed her brutal, alcoholic husband by stabbing, and the 'mercy killers' of pitifully sick relatives can plead diminished responsibility. The offender, often thought to be depressed, is frequently committed to hospital instead of prison. The psychiatric reports are key in these cases.

M̶ ̶ation of sentences because of mental abnormality

Except ̶ ̶ ̶ that it is a fairly small minority, there is no reliable estimate of the number ̶ ̶ffenders who are psychiatrically disordered. Among the male prison populati ̶ ̶ highly selected group, there are:

- 0.6% mentally r̶ ̶led;
- 2% psychotic – mos̶ ̶n associated with violence, especially if paranoid;
- 6% neurotic;
- 10% personality-disordered, ̶ ̶ding psychopathic;
- 12% alcoholic;
- 12% drug-dependent.

A sizeable number are of low intelligence a̶ ̶ ̶cause of this or psychiatric disorder, are socially isolated, unemployed ̶ ̶ ̶homeless. (See Gunn, J, Maden, A, and Swinton, M (1991) 'Treatment ̶ ̶ds of prisoners with psychiatric disorders' *British Medical Journal* 303, 338–4̶ ̶

Women offend far less often and less seriously than ̶ ̶. There are four times as many men convicted as women, and 30 times as ma̶ ̶nt to prison. While women are catching up with men in all areas of crime, sh̶ ̶ting has long been a particularly female offence. While it can be part o̶ ̶ral delinquency, it may also be due to a definite psychiatric disorder. ̶ suffering from anorexia nervosa or young women with bulimia may stea̶ articles that they can well afford, such as chocolate or cheap trinkets. Judges are usually sympathetic. More serious cases are the older women who shoplift persistently.

Case

Lady Isobel Barnett, a favourite on the BBC's Question Time, was convicted in September 1980 of stealing a bottle of milk and a can of tuna from the village shop. This was by no means her first offence. Four days later she committed suicide. She was one of a number of middle-aged, often middle-class, women who shop-lift as a symptom of depression. A convincing psychiatric report is essential for this defence, unhappily not provided for Lady Barnett. Other types of mental disorder which may be relevant to the defence of an offender include:

- schizophrenia;
- mania, hypomania;
- dementia, particularly in early Huntington's chorea, before the diagnosis has been established;
- psychopathic disorder;
- morbid jealousy;
- sequelae of head injury and other organic brain states, eg tumour, multiple sclerosis;
- automatism in epilepsy.

All these conditions are described in detail in later chapters.

False confessions: in some cases they are not accepted; in others they are retracted later.

Case

George Long confessed to the murder of a 14 year old boy in 1978, but was finally cleared in 1995, after 16 years in prison. Psychiatric reports then described him as depressed. He had a long history of mental instability and a reputation for telling fantastic stories, presumably to counteract a feeling that he was of no account.

Long was eventually freed, whereas Timothy Evans had been hanged by the time it was realised that his confession was untrue.

VICTIMS OF TORTURE

A psychiatric assessment is sometimes required by asylum-seekers who claim to have been tortured in the country they have left. Apart from any physical damage, torture may lead to a whole range of symptoms: headache, anxiety sometimes with chronic hyperventilation (overbreathing) and panic, poor sleep and nightmares, poor memory and concentration, depression and post-traumatic stress disorder. A problem for the psychiatrist is gaining the trust of victims.

FITNESS TO DRIVE

An 'At a Glance Guide to the Current Medical Standards of Fitness to Drive' 1966 has been issued by the Drivers' Medical Group of the DVLA, Swansea. Psychiatric disorders listed are:

Psychiatric Disorders	Group 1 Entitlement	Group 2 Entitlement
Neurosis eg Anxiety state/ Depression	DVLA need not be notified. Driving need not cease. Patients must be warned about the possible effects of medication which may affect fitness. However, serious psychoneurotic episodes affecting or likely to affect driving should be notified to DVLA and the person advised not to drive.	Driving should cease with serious *acute* mental illness from whatever cause. Driving may be permitted when the person is symptom free and stable for a period of 6 months. Medication must not cause side effects which would interfere with alertness or concentration. Driving may be permitted also if the mental illness is long-standing but maintained symptom free on small doses of psychotropic medication with no side effects likely to impair driving performance. Psychiatric reports may be required.
Psychosis Schizo-Affective Acute Psychosis Schizophrenia	6 months off the road after an acute episode requiring hospital admission. Licence restored after freedom from symptoms during this period, and the person demonstrates that he/ she complies safely with recommended medication and shows insight into the condition. 1, 2, or 3 year licence with medical review on renewal. Loss of insight or judgment	Recommended refusal or revocation. At least 3 years off driving, during which must be stable and symptom free, and not on major psychotropic or neuroleptic medication, except Lithium. Consultant Psychiatric examination required before restoration of licence, to confirm that there is no residual impairment, the applicant has insight and would be able to recognise if he became unwell. There should be no significant

Psychiatric Disorders	Group 1 Entitlement	Group 2 Entitlement
Psychosis (cont)	will lead to recommendation to refuse/revoke.	likelihood of recurrence. Any psychotropic medication necessary must be of low dosage and not interfere with alertness or concentration or in any way impair driving performance.
Manic depressive psychosis	6–12 months off the road after an acute episode of hypomania requiring hospital admission, depending upon the severity and frequency of relapses. Licence restored after freedom from symptoms during this period and safe compliance with medication. 1, 2, or 3 year licence with medical review on renewal. Loss of insight or judgment will lead to refuse/revoke.	AS ABOVE
Dementia – Organic brain disorders, eg Alzheimer's disease NB: There is no single marker to determine fitness to drive but it is likely that driving may be permitted if there is retention of ability to cope with the general day to day needs of living, together with adequate levels of insight and judgment.	If early dementia, driving may be permitted if there is no significant disorientation in time and space, and there is adequate retention of insight and judgment. Annual medical review required. Likely to be revoked if disorientation in time and space, and especially if insight has been lost or judgment is impaired.	Recommended permanent refusal or revocation if the condition is likely to impair driving performance.

Psychiatric Disorders	Group 1 Entitlement	Group 2 Entitlement
Severe Mental Handicap means a state of arrested or incomplete development of mind which includes severe impairment of intelligence and social functioning.	Severe mental handicap is a *prescribed disability*, licence must be refused or revoked. If stable, mild to moderate mental handicap it may be possible to hold a licence but he/she will need to demonstrate adequate functional ability at the wheel, and otherwise be stable.	Recommended permanent refusal or revocation if severe. Minor degrees of mental handicap when the condition is stable with no medical or psychiatric complications may be able to have a licence. Will need to demonstrate functional ability at the wheel.
Personality Disorder (including post head injury syndrome and psychopathic disorders)	If seriously disturbed such as evidence of violent outbreaks or alcohol abuse and likely to be a source of danger at the wheel, licence would be refused or revoked. Licence restricted after medical reports that behaviour disturbances have been satisfactorily controlled.	Recommended refusal or revocation if associated with serious behaviour disturbance likely to be a source of danger at the wheel. If the person matures and psychiatric reports confirm stability supportive, licence may be permitted/restored. Consultant Pychiatrist report required.

The applicant or licence holder must notify DVLA unless stated otherwise.

NB A person holding entitlement to Group 1 (ie motor car/motor bike) or Group 11 (ie LGV/PCV), who has been relicensed following an acute psychotic episode, of whatever type, should be advised as part of follow up that if the condition recurs, driving should cease and DVLA be notified. General guidance with respect to psychotropic/neuroleptic medication is contained under the appropriate section in the text.

Alcohol and illicit drug misuse/dependency are dealt with under their specific sections.

Reference is made in the introductory page to the current GMC guidance to doctors concerning disclosure in the public interest without the consent of the patient.

ALCOHOL PROBLEMS

Alcohol misuse, with or without dependency: misuse implies a state in which consumption of alcohol causes disturbance of behaviour, alcohol-related disease or other consequences likely to cause harm to the patient, his family or society. He is likely to be drinking more than the national guidelines recommend.

Misuse, confirmed by medical reports, and otherwise unexplained blood test results require a minimum six-month ban from driving, during which controlled drinking should be attained and normal blood tests taken.

Dependency, including fits, requires a one-year driving ban to attain abstinence or controlled drinking. The DVLA must be informed, and for licence restoration it will arrange an independent medical examination and require satisfactory blood results and medical reports from the offender's doctors. The DVLA advises offenders to seek medical and other relevant advice while they are not driving.

Alcohol-related disorders: the DVLA must be informed, and driving is not permitted. Examples include:

- Wernicke's encephalopathy: a mental reaction to severe thiamine deficiency, characterised by confusion, staggering gait and such eye signs as nystagmus.
- Korsakoff's psychosis: usually a sequel to Wernocke's encephalopathy. It comprises an inability to retain any new material, often with confabulation to fill the memory gaps.
- Severe cirrhosis of the liver.

DRUG MISUSE AND DEPENDENCY

Cannabis, Ecstasy, LSD and other hallucinogens and recreational drugs: regular use of these, confirmed by medical enquiry, involves a six-month driving ban. An independent medical assessment and urine screen, arranged by the DVLA, may be required. The DVLA must be kept informed.

Amphetamines, heroin, morphine, *methadone, cocaine and benzodiazepines: regular use or dependency, confirmed by medical enquiry, involves a minimum one year driving ban. For restoration of the licence the DVLA may require an independent medical examination and urine screen, and in any case a favourable report from a consultant or specialist.

Seizures associated with illicit drug use: the DVLA must be informed and may require the patient to be banned from driving for a year. Restoration of the licence requires an independent medical assessment, with urinalysis and a favourable report from the patient's own doctor to confirm that there is no ongoing drug misuse. Patients may also be assessed against the Epilepsy Regulations. They must be told, if their licence is restored, that if they relapse they must stop driving and inform the DVLA Medical Branch.

Note: those taking methadone orally as part of a consultant-supervised withdrawal programme may be licensed subject to annual medical review and a favourable assessment.

CHAPTER TWO

TOOLS FOR THE JOB

The medico-legal practitioner concerned with psychiatric cases requires certain essential equipment: information.

This is of two types:

1 Reliable written authorities on aspects of the law and of psychiatry, for reference.
2 Specific information surrounding the case in question, in the form of statements, records, reports, correspondence and medical notes.

Reference books

Lawyers are often to be seen around the courts laiden with books. Psychiatrists, by contrast, seldom refer to books in their day-to-day practice. For medico-legal work there several books which must be available to the practitioner. They are all published in paperback at reasonable cost, and are worth owning.

Absolutely essential

- The *Diagnostic and Statistical Manual of Mental Disorders* (1994) 4th edn (DSM-IV), American Psychiatric Association.
- 'The International Classification of Diseases', in *Mental and Behavioural Disorders* (1992) 10th edn (ICD-10), World Health Organisation.
- *Mental Health Act Manual* (1996) 5th edn, Sweet and Maxwell.

Highly desirable

- Malcolm Faulk, *Basic Forensic Psychiatry* (1994) 2nd edn, Blackwell Science.
- *Medical Ethics Today* (1996) British Medical Association.

Lawyers and psychiatrists and other health workers need to understand each others' viewpoint and to use the same language in referring to psychological and psychiatric conditions. While everyone except the psychiatrist tends to have his own idea of what is meant by, say, schizophrenia or depression, in legal matters the diagnosis must be accurate and precise and generally accepted.

This is achieved through the use of classificatory systems which lay out categories of mental disorder, and the criteria for specific diagnoses, with clinical descriptions of these, including their natural history. The history can give valuable insights, in some cases, on the person's mental state before any incident and a forecast of the probable outcome. The first may be relevant in matters of competence to make reasonable decisions, criminal responsibility and impairment of function. The second, concerning prognosis, is of particular interest where compensation is involved. It is important to remember, however, that the diagnosis of a particular mental disorder does not necessarily carry any implications as to its cause.

Case

Mrs O, aged 50, developed a major depressive disorder following a hysterectomy which had complications. She was left with a painful, scarred abdomen and mild urinary incontinence. She was suing the Health Authority for the alleged negligence of its servants. Just before she had gone into hospital for the surgery she heard the news that her husband had cancer. Was her mental state precipitated by the operation and its sequelae or by the threat to her husband's well-being and survival?

The psychiatric diagnosis was not in doubt, but its cause left plenty of room for argument.

Historical note

The two great international classificatory systems for mental disorder, the DSM and the ICD mental section, are both approximately 50 years old, but are constantly reviewed and updated. In the 1840 census there was only one category of mental disorder: idiocy/insanity. By 1880 this had increased to seven: mania, melancholia, paresis, dementia, dipsomania, monomania and epilepsy. The purpose of the classification was purely statistical and doctors were not interested. It was the Second World War that gave classification a fillip and related it to clinical practice as well as to statistics. This was because of the large number of soldiers and others affected by psychiatric disorders, with issues of compensation and pensions.

The Veterans Administration of the United States Army developed a much broader nomenclature for psychiatric disorders, while at the same time the World Health Organisation, preparing the sixth revision of its *Classification of Diseases*, included a chapter on mental disorders for the first time. It listed 10 categories of psychosis, nine of psychoneurosis and nine of disorders of character, behaviour and intelligence. However, neither ICD-6 nor the first edition of the *American Diagnostic and Statistical Manual*, DSM-I, made much impact on practitioners, and they were seldom used except for research.

In the late 1970s, DSM-III and ICD-9 were developed in conjunction with each other, the latter coming out in 1978, the former in 1980. They were a vast improvement on the earlier versions, being far more clinically oriented, and the two systems have remained in general use ever since. They both cover the same ground, but with minor differences and both are used internationally. The more widely used of the two, especially in the English-speaking world, is the American DSM.

Both systems were comprehensively reviewed and brought into line with modern psychiatric thinking in the early 1990s as DSM-IV and ICD-10. The compilation of DSM-IV was a team effort, the team numbering more than one thousand. The focus is on clinical research, educational and legal and there is an overriding aim of facilitating communication between professionals in different disciplines concerned with mental health by the use of an official nomenclature, with clear, brief descriptions of each condition.

Organisation of DSM-IV and ICD-10

An outline of the organisational plans of the two systems is useful in locating the part needed.

DSM-IV: the disorders are grouped into 16 major diagnostic classes such as mood disorders, anxiety disorders and schizophrenic and other psychotic disorders. These in turn each comprise between one and 12 or more more precise, usually linked either by similar symptoms or by aetiology. Each diagnosis is coded with a double number. For example, post-traumatic stress disorder (PTSD) is identified as 309.81, the 309 referring to adjustment disorders in general, the 81 to PTSD in particular.

There are two useful appendices:

Appendix A: a diagnostic tree for differentiating between commonly occurring, related conditions. The areas covered are:

- mental disorders due to general medical conditions;
- substance-induced disorders;
- psychotic disorders;
- mood disorders;
- anxiety disorders;
- somatoform disorders, ie with physical symptoms.

Appendix C: a glossary of technical terms in psychiatry.

ICD-10 Chapter V: this contains 10 basic blocks of diagnoses, each block divided up into particular disorders. Each diagnosis is identified, as in DSM-IV, by a two-part number. The first, which is prefixed F, refers to the group of disorders, the second gives the precise identification. In ICD-10 PTSD is coded F43.1. F43 refers to 'reaction to severe stress and adjustment disorders', and the 1 refers to PTSD only. Diagnostic criteria are given.

In both classifications the initials NOS (not otherwise specified) often appear after a diagnosis. Depressive disorder NOS means a disorder with depressive features that do not meet the criteria for major depressive disorder nor for various similar specific disorders.

The value of these internationally recognised classifications for medico-legal work is that they enable the psychiatrist preparing a report to make his diagnosis watertight, while diagnoses used in other psychiatric reports or by plaintiffs and their lawyers can be scrutinised for accuracy in the light of definite criteria.

Case

Mrs Z was a widow of 87 who lived in a hotel in Westgate-on-Sea. She had been left a considerable sum by her late husband. Her nephew, aged 60, was understood to be the main beneficiary in her will. He was concerned to observe that Mrs Z was spending her inheritance rather freely. She frequently made long hire-car trips – for the ride – driven by the hotel proprietor's son and bought quantities of clothes more suitable for a 30 year old. She also purchased a wig. She developed a great interest in a charity for bats, expressed in generous donations.

Seeing his own potential inheritance shrinking fast, the nephew felt convinced that his aunt must have Alzheimer's disease and was no longer competent to manage her own money affairs.

He believed she would be safer in a residential home, with her finances supervised and arranged for a psychogeriatrician to examine her. Her nephew listed numerous instances of her failing mental powers, while the hotel proprietor said that she was just an eccentric old lady. She did not meet the criteria for Alzheimer's disease or any other form of dementia, that is multiple cognitive defects. Her memory was often faulty, but she had none of the other disturbances necessary for the diagnosis, for instance in language or the recognition of various objects.

With no psychiatric grounds, the nephew was unable to prevent Mrs Z from continuing to live in the hotel, taking car journeys and signing her own cheques. Perhaps it was frustration that precipitated the nephew's stroke: in the end he predeceased the old lady.

SOURCES OF SPECIFIC INFORMATION

If a psychiatric assessment is required, it is helpful to have as much information as possible before the psychiatrist examines the plaintiff. The interview can be better focused and the questions more relevant.

Statement of Claim: in medical negligence cases and others involving compensation the first essential is for the psychiatrist is to know precisely what the plaintiff wants, why he thinks the defendant is at fault, and what psychological trauma he believes he has suffered. The Statement of Claim sets this out, and is a better basis than the plaintiff's own account, when it is available.

Medical notes from the hospital involved in negligence cases, and the Accident and Emergency notes plus follow-up hospital notes in cases of accidents at work or on the road are necessary if psychological suffering is claimed. These notes should be scanned for any mention of the patient's state of mind.

Plaintiff's and defendant's statements are used when these are available as are any statements by witnesses, friends or other interested parties. Again, any reference to the plaintiff's mental state is carefully noted, as are any inconsistencies in or between statements.

GP records, going back as far as possible and continuing to the present time are important. The plaintiff's written authority must be obtained for access to these. GP records may provide a mine of information about the patient's medical and psychological history, life-events such as bereavement or divorce at relevant times, and previous injuries or accidents and recovery periods. Any mention of mood is worth noting and prescriptions for hypnotics or psychotropic medication or pain-killers will throw light on the doctor's thinking at the time.

Naturally, the records made after the incident, accident or episode are even more significant. How soon and how often did the patient consult his GP after the event, and what were the complaints? Memory can be deceptive, but the doctor's notes have the value of having been recorded at the time of the patient's visits.

CHAPTER THREE

PREPARING A PSYCHIATRIC REPORT

A common reason for requesting a psychiatric report is for a compensation case involving either medical negligence or employer's negligence, injury or accident. In criminal cases the courts may ask for a psychiatric assessment before sentencing, or a defence lawyer may be seeking mitigation of his client's offence. In cases of violent crime in particular, an assessment of risk may be required. Other situations calling for a psychiatric report include doubts about fitness to plead or to be a competent witness or competence to make decisions, for instance about finances or making a will.

Preparing is the key word in 'preparing a report'. Before writing the report, and preferably before the interview, it is important to have read the Statement of Claim so that you know what aspects of the subject's condition to concentrate on. It also makes good sense to go through all the available documents and records before seeing the plaintiff, providing you with the chronology of events and the opinions of doctors and others involved at the time. This is of particular value when, as so often happens, you are asked to make a psychiatric assessment years after the incident in question.

Crib sheet: aids speed and efficiency. Make a single sheet of notes with key dates and the names of the hospitals, doctors and other staff concerned. A list of bullet points and quotes from the material, all meticulously ascribed and dated is always useful. This means you already have a skeleton of your report when you come to write it.

Putting the subject at ease: it makes it easier to draw information from the person if you are familiar with the basic facts from the start. It is essential to dispel any apprehension the subject may have about the interview. Factual information and especially an account of his emotional reactions flow more easily with an individual who is relaxed. The medical convention of the doctor sitting behind a large desk, as though he were interviewing a prospective employee, can be intimidating and in situations such as this it is worth re-arranging the seating.

If a friend or relative accompanies the subject, make him welcome. It can be illuminating to talk with such a person separately, assuring him that his account and his opinion are valued. It is not advisable to have the friend or relative present during the subject's discussion with you. The presence of the other person is likely to inhibit the patient's frank account and he himself may not be able to resist the temptation to answer questions for the patient or to interrupt the interview.

During the interview you will be making the notes that form the basis of your report. Record as much as you can comfortably, including a few verbatim quotes to provide authenticity, and any visible signs of emotion such as tears, sighs or tremor.

It is quicker and easier if you are able to compose your report soon after the examination, while the interview is still fresh in your mind.

Structuring your report: if you have spent a long time with a verbose individual it is only too easy to write an equally diffuse account. It is also tempting to plunge straight into the key event and the subject's mental state. What is needed is a logically structured presentation, with a regard for chronology.

PLAN FOR A PSYCHIATRIC REPORT

SUBJECT'S FULL NAME

Sentence about what the report is based on: documents, interview with the subject, also with relatives, witnesses or others if available at PLACE/TIME.

BACKGROUND

Family history including deaths, divorces, major illnesses and psychiatric family history if any.

Personal history including birth DATE and PLACE, early health; schools; social and academic achievements, further education; work history.

Psychosexual history including marriage and other relationships, children, and for women, obstetric history.

Past medical history including accidents, injuries, legal cases if any. Operations.

Psychiatric history in detail, including medication and inpatient treatment.

The ACCIDENT or EPISODE or EVENTS leading to the case:

- the circumstances;
- what happened as described by the plaintiff and any others involved;
- the immediate effects.

Sequelae

- physical;
- psychological;
- social and work-related.

CURRENT MENTAL STATE

- from psychological examination, with psychiatric diagnosis;
- implications for the previous mental state;
- prognosis;
- relevance of the accident or alleged negligence, previous psychiatric history and unconnected life events to the subject's mental state.

CONCLUSIONS

Psychiatric and physical state:

- disabilities;
- future outlook with time-scale if possible;
- psychiatric treatment considered necessary or desirable – if any.

Assessment of the causes of psychological and emotional symptoms and the plausibility of the claim.

Note of any special expertise you have relevant to this case, including published work (some practitioners like to start their report with this information).

SIGNATURE

Qualifications

Current post   DATE

Key dates should be placed in the left hand margin throughout.

While this plan is designed for cases where compensation is the main issue, it can be adapted for mitigation or competence matters with particular emphasis on the psychological examination.

Notes on the plan

Background: after the introductory paragraph a major section deals with the subject's family and personal history. Family history is of interest, particularly that of psychiatric illness and of events such as bereavement which could have impinged on the subject's mental state. The time relation between such events and the accident or incident is important. Personal history includes early life – relevant to later reactions – and education and employment – relevant with regard to loss of earning capacity. Psychosexual and past medical history may reveal important occurrences and reactions to them.

Dates are often significant and are anyway essential for producing a coherent whole.

The GP's records can be an excellent source of information, and written, as they are, contemporaneously and dated throughout, they are a check to memory. When a plaintiff complains of symptoms which he relates to the accident or incident, it is of interest to know whether he had experienced similar symptoms previously, which he may now have forgotten. Deliberate deception, like malingering, is very rare, but personal memory is often unreliable. Another useful aspect of the GP's notes is the record of whether and how much the patient complained to the doctor about the pain, disability or depression, which he now remembers as causing him much suffering, immediately after the events and/or lasting a number of months.

The accident or incident: to make this necessarily detailed account easy to read, it is best presented as a coherent story, enhanced where possible by verbatim quotes from the person concerned, medical and other records and correspondence. A psychiatric report need not enter into details about surgical procedures or pathological reports. What must be recorded meticulously is any indication of the person's emotional reactions, even by a chance reference in the medical notes.

In road traffic accidents such matters as alcohol use at the time, the wearing of a seat belt and whether the vehicle had head restraints or an airbag must be mentioned in the report. The age of the vehicles involved is also significant: some of the older, cheaper cars can disintegrate with a relatively minor impact.

In medical cases it is necessary to know how much was explained about the possible complications or side-effects of the treatment, as far as the subject remembers and the medical notes record. Unfortunately, patients do not often concentrate on this aspect of a consultation with a physician.

In surgical cases, similarly, patients give little attention to what they have been told when they sign a consent form for surgery. This failure is compounded if the surgeon has not been thorough and has not made a note of what he did explain to the patient.

After the account of the events which are the subject of the case there should be a section about what happened afterwards, divided into physical, psychological and social and work-related conditions, without, at this stage, attributing causation.

Current mental state: is the next major part of the report. Clinical psychologists frequently employ inventories and questionnaires to demonstrate degrees of, for instance, depression or anxiety. These may appear impressive and scientific, providing an assessment in figures. As a research tool such fill-in forms can be useful in comparing large groups, but in individual compensation cases they are of little value. Since it is obvious which answers will be beneficial to his case, they are bound to become distorted however truthful the plaintiff means to be. The psychiatric assessment depends on eliciting the somatic and other symptoms of psychiatric distress, with the criteria for the different diagnoses clearly in mind. In particular, now that it is so often cited as a symptom, the criteria for post-traumatic stress disorder should be remembered (see Chapter 8).

Conclusions: this includes a description of the subject's present physical and psychological state, related to the claim he is making. The degree of disability – what the person cannot do now that he could do before – needs outlining. It can be difficult to evaluate previous suffering or disability complained of by the subject but from which he has now recovered.

Psychiatric diagnosis is of key importance and also the assessment of prognosis. It is often impossible to give a time-scale for this with any confidence, since it may depend on the patient's physical improvement and unpredictable life events.

Causation in psychiatry is an imprecise concept. Causes are often remote in time from their psychological effects, for instance events in infancy or later childhood may have their effects in later life. Childhood bereavement predisposes to depressive illness in adult life and is then easily triggered. In psychiatry, a single cause may produce several different effects in the same or different people. For example, a divorce may lead to depression, alcoholism, a traffic accident and redundancy, then possibly gambling or crime. Mental handicap may come from one or more of numerous causes, yet appear the same in its end result.

Different schools of though attribute causation very differently. Unlike the case in law, it is meaningless to attempt to be dogmatic in psychiatry.

Case

A 28 year old woman was depressed when her boyfriend cancelled their wedding plans after they were both injured in a car crash. While attending the physiotherapy department, over several months, she formed a relationship with another patient which became serious and her depression lifted.

The final, crucial paragraph in the conclusions is an opinion on the causation of the plaintiff's psychological suffering and what proportion should be ascribed to the incident and what proportion to other events in his life, and any special vulnerabilities.

WHAT IS AT STAKE?

Calculations for compensation come under four heads:
1 Damages for 'pain, suffering and loss of amenity'.
2 Financial loss and expense before the case is concluded.
3 Interest on the above.
4 Future financial loss and expense due to the injury or incident.

Case

A six year old boy suffered cerebral palsy due to obstetric negligence. By far the largest part of the award derived from his projected future loss of earning power and extra living expenses because of his disability.

Until the 20th century, compensation was given almost entirely for physical injury: liability was not accepted for 'nervous' or psychiatric damage. During this century, however, the law has followed, to some extent, the general, gradual increase in the understanding of psychiatric illness and a growing recognition of the possible seriousness of its consequences. Psychiatric illness must be distinguished from normal grief and distress in reaction to adverse events, but when such illness occurs it is likely to produce a loss of function equally as important and worthy of compensation as physical injury. Psychological suffering is as relevant as physical pain.

Case

Mr Ron Lipsius, a musician whose hands were terribly burned during the King's Cross disaster in 1987, was able to claim as much for his psychological agonies as for his burned fingers *per se*.

Psychiatric trauma, unlike physical trauma, can be caused even when the person concerned receives no physical injury.

Case

The first such case, in 1901, was of a Mrs Dulieu who suffered such 'nervous shock' with fear of being injured that she miscarried. A van driver had driven his horse and van into the public house where she was serving behind the bar. She was awarded damages against the company who employed the van driver, although she received no injury – a first!

Much more recently, following the Hillsborough Stadium disaster of 1989, 10 people claimed that they has suffered psychiatrically from seeing the horrific scene on television, knowing that they had friends or relatives there. They won their case on appeal in 1996.

Seven of the prisoners involved in the Strangeways Prison riot put in a claim for damages on psychiatric grounds and the Home Office negotiated an out-of-court settlement with each of them.

Claims for psychiatric trauma and especially post-traumatic stress disorder are currently multiplying and the call for psychiatric assessment is increasing in parallel.

CHAPTER FOUR

VIOLENCE AND THE ASSESSMENT OF DANGEROUSNESS

The problem of violence in our society is currently alarming the public and preoccupying the authorities. Such high profile cases as the massacre of the innocents at Dunblane in 1996 (when 16 children and their teacher were murdered by a paranoid gunman) and the murder of Mr Zito (see p 3) have sharpened awareness, and there has been the advent of new variants on violence: 'road rage' and 'stalking' in their most serious manifestations.

Dangerousness: a definition: 'a propensity to cause serious physical injury or lasting psychological harm to others.' So said the Butler Committee in 1975. It is as good a definition as any, but there can be differences over the meanings of 'serious' and of 'lasting' depending on the mind set of the assessor.

There is an increasing demand for psychiatric reports on violent offenders and the assessment of dangerousness on them and on known psychiatric patients. The calls come from:

1   The courts seeking guidance on sentencing. In May 1996 a new law was introduced giving the judges more powers in detaining psychiatrically disturbed offenders.

2   Mental Health Review Tribunals making decisions about rescinding compulsory orders and allowing the release of detained patients into the community.

3   Hospital managers in relation to the detention of patients under the Mental Health Act of 1983.

4   Parole boards dealing with prisoners.

With the closing down of many of the large psychiatric hospitals, the policy of care in the community has come under the spotlight of public and professional concern. It has highlighted the risk of harm to others from psychiatric patients and emphasised the need for skilled psychiatric assessment with particular reference to the likelihood of future violence, in the short and the longer term.

A Special Working Party of the Royal College of Psychiatrists has been examining the problems and in 1996 published a 13-page booklet, *Assessment and Clinical Management of Risk of Harm to Other People*. This points out that such risk cannot be completely eliminated since it is in part dependent on unpredictable and changing circumstances. It is also important that due weight is given to professional psychiatric opinion in comparison with that of laypeople, however well-intentioned.

Case

Glen Grant, a violent rapist, spent 10 years in Broadmoor Special Hospital followed by a rehabilitative period at Cane Hill, an ordinary psychiatric hospital. He was discharged in 1996 by the decision of a lay panel but against psychiatric advice. Four days later he made a brutal attack on a young woman in her home.

Psychiatric patients, as opposed to sane criminals, if they are ill enough to pose a threat to others, are likely themselves to be vulnerable to harm and in need of psychiatric help on that account too. They run an enhanced risk of suicide, self-mutilation, self-neglect or exploitation.

THE ASSESSMENT OF DANGEROUSNESS

The key essential is information, as wide-ranging and detailed as possible. Outside sources include family, social services, police, doctor and a psychiatrist involved at any time, and in certain circumstances school reports and employers' assessments.

Risk factors in the history

- previous violence, including suicidal behaviour;
- absence of regret;
- absence of provocation before the violence;
- repeated impulsive behaviour;
- inability to cope with stress or delay gratification;
- rootlessness;
- lack of friends;
- lack of support;
- culture of violence in social background;
- alcohol misuse;
- illegal drug use;
- paranoid beliefs;
- deceptiveness;
- threats of violence;
- poor compliance with treatment previously.

PERSONAL DATA OF RELEVANCE

Childhood experience

- sick, neglectful or psychiatrically disturbed parents;
- disturbed early relationship with mother, failure of bonding;
- alcoholic, absent or violent father;
- early emergence of anti-social traits.

Any of these factors tends to be associated with later delinquent, including violent, behaviour. Physical or sexual abuse in childhood often lies in the background of those who become persistently violent, including mutilation of their victims and homicide.

Case

Tom, aged four months, was taken to hospital by his parents who said he had fallen out of his cot. The infant had a fractured skull, two limb fractures and multiple bruises. His injuries were consistent with his having been swung round against the wall. This was clearly a case of what is known as 'non-accidental injury'. Tom's father was convicted of manslaughter but the facts of his own childhood were put forward in mitigation of the offence. He had been grossly neglected by a drunken mother as a young child and then brought up in care. In the children's home he was subjected to sexual abuse for a number of years. The effect had been to produce a man unable to feel affection, a psychopathic personality with poor impulse control. He was sent to a psychiatric hospital for treatment rather than to prison.

Psychosexual history

Violent sexual offenders typically show an inability to form stable sexual relationships and often have a history of sadistic fantasies which may later be acted out. Careful, sensitive and sympathetic questioning is essential for eliciting these underlying factors. Absolute refusal to talk about sexual feelings and ideas is usually an ominous sign, as is failure to co-operate with therapy following an offence in the past.

An abnormal, usually intense relationship with his mother may set up a paradoxical resentment to all women, or a rebuff at a critical age may induce a hatred of them. A man may only attack women with, for instance, red hair, if his early humiliating experience involved a red-haired woman.

Some jealousy is normal in a sexual relationship, and some homosexual pairing in particular can be associated with violence. Excessive jealousy without cause, morbid or pathological jealousy, can be extremely dangerous for the other partner: there are several psychiatric conditions which may underlie it.

Rape: most rapists are not mentally ill, although occasionally a manic patient may commit the offence. Types of rapist:

- aggressive anti-social;
- aggressive sadistic;
- explosive impulsive.

Paedophiles who have never, since puberty, experienced sexual urges towards adults of either sex are more dangerous than the less exclusive type. Older men – women are hardly ever involved – are less likely to be violent than those under the age of 35. One type of paedophile likes children and only harms them when he is at risk of discovery; the other dislikes the children he bribes with sweets or money and uses them callously and sadistically.

Case

Donald was 23, a failure at school and now jobless. He was a disappointment to his sports enthusiast, heavy-drinking father. Donald was undersized and this was exaggerated by a marked idiopathic scoliosis. No girl would look at him but his short stature was no disadvantage with young children. He spent a lot of time outside the local primary school, watching the children in the playground. He thought he had made a friend in one boy and showed him his pornographic pictures. The youngster called him 'a dirty old perve' and said he would inform on him. Donald strangled him in panic, to shut him up. There was no case for mitigation.

Areas of interest to provide a pyschological background to dangerousness include:

Work history

- dismissals and the reasons for them;
- attitude to authority;
- relationships with colleagues or workmates;
- ability to co-operate harmoniously with others;
- disagreements, fights;
- unemployment and the reasons for it.

Personality

- isolated or outgoing;
- placid or tense;

- 'chip on the shoulder';
- friendly or aloof;
- touchy or easygoing;
- confrontational;
- egocentric or sympathetic to others;
- reaction to criticism: degree of self-esteem;
- short fuse or over-controlled.

Medical history

Conditions of interest include:

- Road traffic accident or other cause of serious head injury, leading to an organic personality syndrome. This is recognised by the law and can involve recklessly disinhibited behaviour and episodes of rage with the most trivial cause.
- Epilepsy, particularly that affecting the temporal lobe is occasionally associated with violence: this is usually in the period following a fit.
- Electroencephalographic abnormalities without seizures are sometimes associated with violence.
- Diabetes mellitus with poor control may be relevant to violent attacks under the confusing and disinhibiting effects of hypoglycaemia: abnormally low blood sugar.
- It is also worth enquiring for a history of premenstrual tension, a diagnosis which has excused some women from acts of violence. Presumably it carries a risk of further violence each month.

Psychiatric history

- A family history of psychiatric illness or alcoholism is of interest.
- Details of any psychiatric illness suffered by the subject, with reference to symptoms and behaviour, attitude to treatment and clinical response.

Mental state at the interview

Assessment of:

- mood state, eg depressed, angry, frightened, tense;
- suspiciousness;
- hallucinations, especially voices telling the subject what to do;
- delusions, particularly of a persecutory nature;

- intelligence;
- inconsistencies in the subject's account.

Psychiatric conditions which may lead to violence

- anti-social personality (psychopathy) which may also be accompanied by paranoid ideas or depression;
- schizophrenia, paranoid type;
- manic-depressive illness, either phase;
- other depressive illness;
- other paranoid states, eg morbid jealousy, which affects men mainly, with obsessional searching for 'evidence' and may lead to homicide (alcoholism may be involved), drug-induced paranoia and, rarely, the Capgras syndrome in which the patient sees his loved ones replaced by impostors, whom he may attack.

Violent episodes

- One violent offence carries a 14% chance of reconviction.
- Four violent offences mean a 60% likelihood of repetition.
- Actual bodily harm (ABH) may have been intended as grievous bodily harm (GBH) or murder.

Details of the violence

- was the victim a particular person?
- were threats made?
- persecutory delusions?
- auditory hallucinations, especially the 'command' type?
- had the person discontinued prescribed medication?
- had he shown increased irritability recently?
- provocation or expectation of gain by the violence?

Hoped for effects of treatment

Mentally ill: reduction of anger and tension; reduction in psychotic symptoms, such as delusions, hallucinations, some insight into the fact of illness.

Mentally impaired: less aggressive, less anti-social behaviour; increased sociability with others.

Anti-social personality disorder: improved behaviour; improved emotional reactions to other people; less egocentric attitude; better acceptance of authority and toleration of frustration; improved impulse control, especially in sexual offenders.

The response to treatment is vitally important for assessing dangerousness. Alcohol or drugs are often involved and the offender's companions may have influenced him. Fatigue can lead to irritability and violence, and psychotic symptoms are frequently denied or concealed and are missed.

Family violence

Victims may be:

- children, especially young ones: non-accidental injury, older children: sexual abuse.
- partners, usually females.
- elderly relatives.

Common ingredients are alcohol and anti-social personality disorder.

Assessment of dangerousness is so important that wherever possible the responsibility should be shared among several professionals.

CHAPTER FIVE

PHYSICAL SYMPTOMS FROM PSYCHOLOGICAL CAUSES

Body and mind are ineradicably attached, each affecting the state of the other. Francis Bacon in 1605 invited us to consider 'how, and how farre the humours and affects of the body do alter and work upon the mind: or again, how and how farre the passions and apprehensions of the mind do alter and work upon the bodie'. At its most dramatic, a state of acute anxiety induced by the sight of a burglar may trigger a fatal heart attack, and it is established statistically that the depression of bereavement is associated with an increased risk of cancer and cardiovascular disease.

The term 'psychosomatic', coined more than 150 years ago, is now unfashionable but the modern classificatory systems both include sections on 'somatoform disorders'. These refer to physical manifestations symptomatic of some psychological conditions. In this area, however, the diagnoses and criteria laid down in the *International Classification of Disease and the Diagnostic and Statistical Manual* (ICD-10 and DSM-IV) are unhelpful in practice. Yet in cases involving legislation and compensation it is of the utmost relevance to distinguish between the direct effects of an accident or negligence and symptoms caused or enhanced by a pre-existing psychological disorder.

Case

At the time of the accident Mr G, aged 42, with a young family and a mortgage, had been in a state of chronic anxiety because of the threat of redundancy as his firm was being progressively down-sized. The car accident, for which the other driver was clearly to blame, caused Mr G a mild whiplash injury (his seat had a head-restraint). This he would have been expected to recover from completely within six months or less, but two years later Mr G was still suffering neck pain and limitation of movement. This interfered with his ability to work. The medico-legal argument centred on whether and how much the persistence of his symptoms was contributed to by his ongoing state of anxiety. The case was finally settled at a figure considerably lower than Mr G's solicitors had originally hoped for.

PAIN

This is the symptom most frequently presented to both surgeons and physicians and often the most important in compensation cases. It causes distress and suffering and in many cases a secondary loss of function: it is difficult to perform a movement associated with pain. The difficulty with assessing pain is that it is a purely subjective experience and can only be diagnosed from the patient's account and sometimes such learned behaviours as groaning, weeping, grimacing and increased muscle tension.

Acute pain usually has an organic cause and is dealt with quickly. It is chronic and recurrent pain that exercise medico-legal practitioners and pain which is most likely to be in part or wholly psychogenic. Depression, anxiety, chronic tension and panic all increase a patient's vulnerability to pain, and any pain already present is made worse. Pain can, in itself, be a symptom of a psychological disorder, replacing a painful emotion. The patient may appear to be cheerful and brave despite unfortunate life circumstances, only complaining of pain – in the limbs, abdomen, head or chest. It is more acceptable for the patient's self-image, particularly in some personalities, to complain of what is assumed to be a physical symptom than to admit to a feeling of fear or despair.

Anti-depressants, especially the older tricyclic formulations, such as amitriptyline, are as efficacious as analgesics in these cases.

Specific pain syndromes

Those without an identifiable organic cause.

Back pain: This is probably the most commonly occurring and troublesome pain and it is usually difficult to disentangle minor physical events and psychological factors in the production of the symptom. X ray investigation is negative apart from the inevitable early signs of age-related degeneration in the lumbar and cervical regions of those over 35 years of age.

Case

Mrs P was 45 and worked as a care assistant in a small private nursing home for the elderly and was often called upon to do heavy lifting. She suffered crippling backache which came on suddenly one night and did not abate. Her doctor and her friends thought the back pain must have been caused by lifting the heavier patients and that her employers were culpable since they had provided neither mechanical hoists nor staff instruction in lifting techniques. Mrs P could no longer cope with her job, yet she had no other training with which to earn a living at her age.

Focusing on the events in her life in the period leading up to the onset of the back symptoms, it emerged that Mrs P's husband, who was some years older than she was, had recently been diagnosed as having a prostate cancer, while her elderly mother seemed to be developing Alzheimer's disease. The double burden was more than Mrs P could bear. She became depressed, with poor sleep, poor appetite and the back pain. The back pain she could blame on her working conditions and feel righteously angry. Monetary gain was a likely outcome. It was difficult to argue that her personal circumstances may not have played a large part in causing the continuing back pain, and Mrs P settled for £50,000.

Pelvic pain: this is another common syndrome which is frequently psychologically mediated. Sometimes it is caused by pelvic inflammatory disease but more often there is no evidence of organic pathology. Laparoscopy and ultrasound are excellent diagnostic aids. Psychogenic pelvic pain is liable to develop when there is sexual or relationship conflict, and dyspareunia can be an indication of this. In an unhappy woman with a difficult partner any minor gynaecological procedure, for instance sterilisation or removal of a cervical polyp may, if there is any hint of a complication, may cause the onset of the syndrome of pelvic pain.

Pelvic pain, whether organic or psychosomatic, is often accompanied by tiring backache.

The claim to have suffered sexual abuse in childhood is put forward in some cases of pelvic pain, but is difficult to substantiate. For a more detailed discussion, see Fry (1993).

Headache: chronic or recurrent headache, apart from migraine, is usually of the tension type: a dull, generalised feeling of pressure round the head. It is likely to be the response to ongoing stress, but when it arises or becomes more severe after a minor head injury the original stressor is often forgotten. The injury is seen as the sole cause, and a legal case may be brought.

Post-traumatic neurosis is a common sequel to a relatively minor, closed head injury. The syndrome is characterised by a diffuse, persistent headache, which is resistant to analgesics, and also dizziness and a light-headed feeling, irritability, restlessness, visual difficulties, lack of concentration, impaired confidence and a low mood. There are no physical signs, but the syndrome is well-established as brought on by minor head injury. However, it is aggravated by work or domestic stress and worry, eyestrain, a noisy environment, and lack of emotional support.

Facial pain: atypical facial pain, not the neuralgic type, is another pain syndrome which is commonly a symptom of depression. It may affect the temporomandibular joint – temporomandibular arthralgia – or present as a deep, throbbing pain. The teeth are often wrongly blamed and this is particularly likely if there has been a recent dental operation. The dentist may be sued if the smallest detail of the procedure was at fault.

AUTONOMIC DYSFUNCTION

An important group of psychogenic symptoms is mediated through the autonomic nervous system: that which controls automatically such vital functions as breathing, heartbeat and digestion. The patient complains of physical symptoms and usually fails to connect them with his emotional state. This is particularly likely in the case of chronic tension, stress and worry. Depression may also be a causative factor.

Cardiovascular symptoms

- increased heart rate;
- palpitations;
- discomfort in the left chest area;
- awareness of missed beats;
- throbbing in the neck;
- chest pain (radiating down the left arm or up to the jaw, if the patient has heard of these as symptoms of a heart disease);
- blood pressure may be raised temporarily with an increased heart rate, and if the patient knows that it is raised he may experience headaches and dizziness.

Respiratory symptoms

- feeling of constriction in the chest;
- difficulty in breathing in (in contrast to the asthmatic's difficulty in breathing out);
- shortness of breath, with or without exertion.

The hyperventilation syndrome: fast, shallow breathing is part of a normal autonomic response to an anxiety-provoking situation or in states of anxiety. It is usually short-lived and only occurs occasionally. In some people, however, of perfectionist personality and chronically or easily made tense, hyperventilation attacks are frequent and may produce alarming symptoms, for example pins and needles, tremors, muscular spasms and even fits. Washing out the arterial carbon dioxide through the abnormal breathing leaves the nerve cells too alkaline, and hyperirritable. Overactivity of the sympathetic side of the autonomic system produces tachycardia, palpitations, nausea and diarrhoea, frequent urination and excessive sweating. Relative shortage of oxygen may manifest in dizziness and altered consciousness.

It is difficult for the patient and his relatives to realise that these symptoms are not part of a genuine, serious illness.

Genitourinary symptoms

- frequent passing of water;
- urgency;
- lack of libido;
- failure of erection;
- menstrual discomfort and irregularity;
- difficulties with intercourse.

Nervous symptoms

- pins and needles and prickling sensations;
- tinnitus;
- blurred vision;
- dizziness (not vertigo, ie no sense of rotation);
- fatigue;
- poor concentration.

Gastrointestinal symptoms

- difficulty in swallowing;
- dry mouth;
- wind;
- borborygmi (tummy rumbles);
- frequent loose motions, irritable colon;
- digestive discomfort.

CHRONIC FATIGUE SYNDROME

Persistent, disabling fatigue is a common additional complaint among patients bringing compensation cases. They find themselves exhausted by the mildest physical or mental exertion and even feel fatigued at rest. Usually they have difficulty in concentrating and sometimes have muscular aching.

While in some cases of this syndrome there may be a viral origin, psychological factors, especially depression, are always involved.

Checklist for diagnosing chronic fatigue syndrome

A Either (or both) of the following must be present:

- persistent and distressing complaints of feelings of exhaustion after minor mental effort (such as performing or attempting to perform everyday tasks that do not require unusual mental effort);
- persistent and distressing complaints of feelings of fatigue and bodily weakness after minor physical effort.

B At least one of the following symptoms must be present:

- feelings of muscular aches and pains and weakness;
- dizziness;
- tension headaches;
- sleep disturbance;
- inability to relax;
- irritability.

C The patient is unable to recover from the symptoms in criterion A by means of rest, relaxation or entertainment.

D The duration of the disorder is at least three months, preferably six.

E Exclusions: this syndrome should not be diagnosed in the presence of mood disorders, panic disorder, generalised anxiety disorder, post-concussional syndrome, postencephalitic syndrome or organic emotional lability disorder.

Treatment with anti-depressants of the serotonin re-uptake inhibiting type (SSRIs) are sometimes helpful, especially if tension and depression are prominent. Graduated exercise is essential in the syndrome presenting with muscle pain and weakness.

Case

Mrs P had a cholecystectomy and the scar became infected, was slow to heal and did not look neat. Mrs P brought a case against the surgeon, the most costly part to her being the disabling, persistent fatigue she suffered afterwards, preventing her from returning to work for two years. The psychiatrist examining her felt that she was suffering from a depressive illness and that this underlay her chronic fatigue syndrome. On inquiry he found that she had been depressed before the operation, following the death of her 16 year old son in a motorbike accident.

MUSCULOSKELETAL SYMPTOMS

The musculoskeletal system is the largest in the body and is involved in all forms of physical activity from championship tennis to playing a Beethoven piano sonata. It is particularly vulnerable to damage in road traffic and other accidents.

The symptoms are:

- pain;
- stiffness;
- limitation of movement.

This combination is capable of producing severe disability, and leading to numerous compensation cases. The areas to assess are:

- immediate pain and suffering and disability;
- psychological effect of the trauma if the accident was alarming;
- time off work, especially for sportspersons;
- effect on the subject's leisure activities, eg gardening, DIY, dancing;
- possible impairment in sexual activity, affecting relationship;
- continuing pain.

Backache is especially common and is dealt with on p 42. Chronic neck and shoulder pain and a syndrome of generalised muscle pain are seen frequently in medico-legal practice. Both conditions tend to arise in, and be maintained by, a depressive mood.

Once a musculoskeletal problem has become established, there is a self-perpetuating cycle of pain, muscular tension and poor sleep, associated in turn with fatigue and irritability. Whiplash injuries often cause the onset of musculoskeletal syndrome, but recovery within a few months is the norm unless some psychological disorder prevents it. A limp is often retained long after the other symptoms have subsided: this has often become a habit.

Repetitive strain injury (RSI)

RSI was first diagnosed in Australia in the early 1980s. It is now seen often in keyboard operators as the subject of litigation. The symptoms are pain and weakness in the arms, and sometimes headache, backache and dizziness. Psychological factors are almost certainly involved and few people who develop RSI are happy in their work. There is an area of conflict between those who consider this a purely physical disorder and those who believe in a major emotional contribution to the aetiology.

Writer's cramp is a condition with several similarities, but is seen less often nowadays. It is fitting that penpusher's disorder has been ousted, in this technological age, by word processor's RSI. Musicians, who also use their small muscles in a concentrated fashion, have long suffered from a condition involving a painful inability to use their arms and fingers with precision. Perhaps they, too, suffer physically because of fine repetitive movements in addition to the input of performance anxiety.

Case

Philip was a concert violinist. To survive in his competitive world he had to practice eight hours a day keeping the classics well-polished and learning something new and modern for each concert in addition. An added strain was the recent unfaithfulness of his much younger partner.

This was the situation at the time of the accident when a waiter with a tray carelessly let go of a swing door when Philip was coming through, carrying his violin case and music. The edge of the door caught the little finger of Philip's right hand, causing bruising. Although the marks disappeared in two or three weeks, the finger remained stiff and painful and he could not play. He was awarded damages but the amount was almost certainly modified by the psychiatric report.

MALINGERING

The term means the fraudulent simulation or exaggeration of symptoms for the purpose of gain. Lawyers are prone to believe that it is not uncommon, and there are well-documented cases of patients who have claimed to be unable to walk, who have subsequently been captured on video making shopping trips. In practice, malingering is extremely unusual. Patients may exaggerate their sufferings when there is litigation under consideration, but they are likely to have convinced themselves of the truth of their claims and are not deliberately trying to deceive.

Malingering is a diagnosis to avoid. It is better to make a meticulous evaluation of the patient's symptoms, his circumstances and his mental state and let the facts speak for themselves.

CHAPTER SIX

PSYCHOLOGICAL EFFECTS FROM PHYSICAL DISORDERS

Any physical injury or disease produces some kind of emotional response. It may be mild and disregarded as normal, or a disabling illness in itself. In a minority of cases the psychological symptoms are the earliest indication of an impending physical disorder. From the medico-legal point of view, it is important to distinguish between primary psychiatric symptoms and those due to a physical injury or insult.

For example, after sustaining an injury in a road traffic accident, the victim may feel a little apprehensive about driving again. This is normal and natural. It is more serious if he is paralysed with fear when he sits in the driving seat and cannot even start the engine. It is worse still if his employment demands that he should drive. In this situation compensation issues are likely to arise.

Psychiatric symptoms due to physical causes

Anxiety: the hallmark of neurosis, according to Freud, it is extremely common, and is often associated with depression. It shows itself in three ways:

- *Psychological*: inner feelings of apprehension, fear or panic, sometimes with psychomotor immobilisation, as in the case of the driver above. Aggressive impulses or a sensation of unreality may accompany the fear.
- *Intellectual*: difficulty in concentrating, inability to think logically and constructively and unreliable memory.
- *Bodily*: any of these: palpitations, chest pain, sweating, frequent urination and less often, diarrhoea, tremor, headache, blurred vision, fainting and hyperventilation.

Anxiety may be acute, including panic attacks and unreasonable phobias of everyday situations, places or objects. Chronic anxiety is characterised by distressing disturbances of mood, inability to cope with the normal activities of life and work, fatigue, difficulty in getting to sleep and an increase or decrease in appetite. Obsessional checking may be a symptom of chronic anxiety.

Medical causes of anxiety

- *Neurological*, 25%, including the sequelae to concussion or other head injury, cerebral vascular disorders, multiple sclerosis, brain tumour and some forms of epilepsy.

- *Endocrine*, 25%, including hyper- and hypothyroidism, ovarian or testicular dysfunction, pituitary disease, hypoglycaemia in diabetes and phaeochromocytoma.
- *Chronic infections*, 12%, including malaria, atypical viral pneumonia, viral hepatitis and glandular fever.
- *Rheumatic*, 12%, including rheumatoid arthritis, systemic lupus erthymatosis, temporal arteritis.
- *Circulatory*, 12%, anaemia, cerebral anoxia from any cause, paroxysmal tachycardia and coronary insufficiency.
- *Others* include malignant disease, nephritis, Meniere's disease, reactions to medication, especially in the elderly.

Post-traumatic stress disorder (PTSD), which appears regularly in medico-legal cases, involves a large element of fear. Because of its importance, Chapter 7 is dedicated to the disorder.

The symptoms of anxiety can be so obvious and dramatic that it is tempting to attribute them to some upsetting event such as an accident or medical negligence and fail to take proper account of non-specific physical findings which would lead to the diagnosis of an underlying physical disorder.

Case

Mr Y, 53 and overweight, had always been something of a hypochondriac. It was no surprise that he should be very anxious before his operation for benign prostatic enlargement, continually asking if it was cancer. After the surgery he recovered well medically, but seemed unusually uncommunicative and withdrawn. It was thought that he was still worried about his health, and he was referred to a psychiatrist. Mr Y categorically denied being anxious or depressed or brooding over the possibility of cancer. He seemed, indeed, remote and unconcerned, and gave oddly short, superficial answers to the doctor's questions. It emerged that he did not know the day, the date or the name of the hospital.

Mr Y was suffering from an organic brain disorder, not merely a neurosis. He had atherosclerosis with cerebral ischaemia, probably leading to a mild thrombotic episode. It is regrettable that nearly 70% of psychiatrists fail to give their patients a physical examination. This can involve delay in the diagnosis of organic disease, or its being overlooked until some crisis occurs.

Depression: depression can mean a low mood or a definite psychiatric illness, and with anxiety is one of the reactions most likely to be associated with physical illness (p 55). It is also the psychiatric condition most likely to be produced by an as yet undetected physical disorder. Depressive illness can be mild, moderate or severe and basically reactive, or severe with psychotic symptoms. In the latter case there may be an underlying hereditary tendency and recent life-events become less relevant. Depression may show itself in any of these ways:

- sad, hopeless mood, often beyond tears;
- feeling of worthlessness;
- indecisiveness;
- slowing down of thought, movement, speech and activity;
- in a minority of cases, usually elderly, a state of agitation and ineffectual restlessness;
- loss of concentration, libido, initiative and interest in usual pursuits;
- loss of appetite, with weight loss;
- insomnia;
- lack of confidence;
- in psychotic depression: delusions of guilt or persecution, hallucinations of accusing voices or dead relatives.

Medical conditions associated with reactive depression

- myocardial infarction, angina, congestive heart failure;
- transient cerebral ischaemia, transient ischaemic attack (TIA), stroke, anaemia;
- loss of sight, hearing or sensation;
- cancer;
- arthritis, diabetes, some kinds of epilepsy, sarcoid, HIV infection.

Medication that can cause depression

- *psychotropic*: eg antipsychotics, benzodiazepine anxiolytics and hypnotics, chlormethiazole, fenfluramine (appetite suppressant);
- *cardiovascular*: eg beta-blockers, central hypotensives, methyldopa, digoxin;
- *steroids and hormones*: eg prednisolone, oral contraceptives, oestrogens, progestogens, cyproterone, clomiphene;
- *analgesics and anti-inflammatories*: eg opiates, indomethacin, ibuprofen;
- *antihistamines*: eg chlorpheniramine;
- *neurological*: eg anti-convulsant, anti-Parkinsonian, bromocriptine, baclofen;
- *antibacterial and anti-fungal*: eg penicillins, sulphonamides, tetracyclines, metronidazole, ketoconazole, griseofulvin;

- *antineoplastic*: eg cisplatin, vincristine, azathioprine;
- *others*: disulfiram, salbutamol, ranitidine, methysergide.

Of course, not everyone taking these medicines becomes depressed; those most likely to be affected are the constitutionally vulnerable who may have had previous depressive episodes.

Surgical operations associated with depression of either type

That is, any that are perceived by the patient as mutilating, for example:
- hysterectomy;
- mastectomy, lumpectomy;
- amputation of a limb;
- removal of a testicle;
- scarring after surgery.

Case

Mr B, aged 25, had a successful operation for testicular cancer, but hanged himself when he had to reveal his loss to a girlfriend. His parents claimed that the surgeon should have foreseen the risk of this outcome and had been negligent in failing to arrange psychological support and supervision for their son. They lost the case. Presumably the judge did not consider that an operation which had saved the man from certain death could reasonably have been expected to lead to his suicide.

Medical conditions associated with agitated or psychotic depression

- cancer of the pancreas, lymphoma;
- hypothyroidism;
- encephalitis;
- mononucleosis, influenza, viral hepatitis;
- kidney failure;
- cirrhosis of the liver;
- pernicious anaemia.

Some medicines may also be responsible for this type of depression, for instance methyldopa, propranolol, clonidine, corticosteroids, mefloquine, chloroquine, phenylbutazone.

Demoralisation: this is distinct from depression, but a common, distressing psychological condition resulting from various injuries and illnesses, especially those likely to be of medico-legal interest. The central feature is the subject's altered self-image, with dramatic loss of self-confidence, increased dependency and increasingly limited activity, and lack of enjoyment in anything. Sleep and appetite are unaffected, unlike the situation in depression.

Conditions often associated with demoralisation

- heart attack;
- cancer;
- burns;
- amputation, breast or facial surgery;
- stroke;
- any chronic, socially debilitating disease, eg diabetes, sickle cell anaemia, epilepsy, ulcerative colitis.

Dementias which can produce depression

- multi-infarct type;
- Alzheimer's disease, an early manifestation;
- Jacob-Creutzfeldt disease;
- cerebral sarcoid;
- chronic organo-phosphate reaction – frequently the basis of a claim.

Pseudo-depression: some of the symptoms of physical disease can be mistaken for those of depression. Distinguishing features are as follows:

- in depression the patient loses interest in his usual pursuits, while in physical illness it is the energy which is lacking;
- in depression the patient gives up on and bemoans his difficulties, while in physical illness he tries to cover up for his weakness and continues to make an effort;
- in depression the patient often blames other people, while in physical illness he is apologetic for not being able to do things;
- the depressive is usually unable to sleep properly, although he may spend an abnormally long time in bed, while the physically ill person sleeps from exhaustion;
- weight loss is common to both conditions, but while lack of interest in food may affect the depressed individual, the physically ill one may retain a normal appetite and still lose weight;
- anti-depressants usually help with depression but not with physical illness.

Hysterical symptoms: hysteria is an unfashionable diagnosis and best avoided if possible. Nevertheless, there are some cases in which nothing else is appropriate. The 19th century hysterical patients converted their emotional conflicts into major symptoms, such as blindness, paralysis or aphonia. Today the hysterical symptom is more likely to be pain and thus is difficult to test.

Case

Miss T was in her twenties. She worked as a secretary at a university, and was romantically attached to her boss and craved his admiration. When the new computer system was introduced with minimal information, Miss T could not master is complexities. It was then that she developed what she referred to as RSI – repetitive strain injury – which was at that time receiving a lot of publicity. Miss T suffered paralysing pain in her neck and right arm, which became rigid at the sight of the Pentium computer. She struggled visibly but unavailingly to force her fingers onto the keyboard, but the pain and muscle spasm were too severe. It was obvious that she could not possibly do her work and that this was not her fault.

The boss was gratifyingly concerned (because he feared an epidemic of RSI). Miss T was removed from keyboard work and given light other duties. She was not unhappy and was not, of course, aware of the mechanism underlying her symptoms.

The meaning of symptoms: Miss T's case illustrates what a particular symptom can mean to the individual. Her neck and arm pain meant escape from a difficult work situation and the bonus of sympathy from her colleagues. A similar pain affecting a violinist or a fast bowler could mean a missed match or concert, or even a blighted career.

Surgery to remove a cancerous lump in the breast might give a welcome sense of relief to one woman, but mean devastating damage to her sexual attractiveness for another. Similarly, a scar on the face could even be a source of pride to a particular type of man, but the mark of a small incision at the back of the knee was extremely upsetting to a young woman who demanded compensation for her 'spoilt appearance'.

PSYCHOLOGICAL SYMPTOMS WHICH MAY BE THE HARBINGERS OF IMPENDING PHYSICAL ILLNESS

Anxiety may be the first indication of:
- stroke;
- respiratory failure in obstructive airways disease, pneumonia;
- myocardial infarction;

- early dementia, whether Alzheimer's or multi-infarct type;
- hyperthyroidism;
- hypoglycaemia;
- withdrawal from alcohol or drugs.

The agitated depression of hypothyroidism may be mistaken for an anxiety state.

The symptoms of anxiety include:

- rapid heart rate, perhaps palpitations;
- tremor;
- sweating;
- difficulty in getting to sleep and staying asleep;
- frequency of passing water;
- poor concentration.

Depression is frequently the first indication of:

- lung cancer, breast cancer and other malignancy;
- Alzheimer's disease;
- liver failure, for instance in alcoholic cirrhosis;
- hypothyroidism;
- brain tumour;
- anaemia;
- Cushing's syndrome.

The symptoms of depression, which is usually of the reactive type, are:

- low mood, inability to feel pleasure;
- lowered vitality;
- loss of interest in normal affairs;
- poor sleep, poor appetite;
- poor concentration.

Delusional beliefs: those about the patient's own body may be symptomatic of psychotic depression or schizophrenia, but they may also have a basis in reality. A depressive who believes that his bowels are permanently blocked or rotting away may have a cancer of the colon. A schizophrenic complaining of rats gnawing his feet in the night may be suffering from diabetic ischaemia.

Misdiagnosis of a psychiatric disorder and the application of a psychiatric label to a medically ill patient is a disaster. It delays appropriate treatment and reduces the chances of recovery. If the delay is considerable the patient may have grounds for a claim of medical negligence.

Case

Mr S developed psychotic symptoms at the age of 28, with paranoid delusions and outbursts of shouting and violence. He was admitted to a psychiatric unit with a diagnosis of acute schizophrenia. His symptoms gradually subsided with substantial doses of a major tranquilliser and he was discharged on a maintenance dose. Two months later his condition deteriorated. He now had visual hallucinations and a curious difficulty in assessing the passage of time. He was readmitted and a junior doctor who had come from a neurology firm took a particular interest in Mr S and found his performance on intellectual testing patchily impaired.

A CT scan was arranged and a deep-seated tumour in the left temporal area was detected. Mr S's wife made a formal complaint and medical negligence proceedings are now under way.

Some specific physical illnesses and their psychiatric concomitants

Hyperthyroidism is almost always associated with psychiatric symptoms, typically feelings of apprehension, restlessness, distractibility and labile emotions.

Features that distinguish it from simple anxiety are warm dry palms, rather than cold and damp, and a pulse rate that remains rapid during sleep.

Hypercortisolism from Cushing's disease or syndrome involves depression in a third of cases, while others are manic or have the symptoms of delirium.

Hypothyroid symptoms may be mistaken for depression: weakness, low libido, low mood and slowed speech, but there are likely also to be such other symptoms as deafness, paraesthesiae, dry skin and hair. All symptoms get better with hormone replacement.

Diabetes mellitus and its early manifestations, such as fatigue, anorexia, polyuria and blurred vision may be misread as neurotic, while hypoglycaemia, if it arises, can mimic the signs of anxiety. The patient appears nervous, pale, sweaty and tremulous and actually feels anxious. Paranoid thinking and hallucinations may develop if the condition is unchecked.

Strokes especially if they affect the non-dominant, right side of the brain, are commonly associated with a depression which responds to anti-depressant therapy. Severe, or repeated minor cerebrovascular accidents lead to a stepwise progression into dementia.

Diffuse vascular disease such as atherosclerosis, can cause subtle intellectual deterioration, personality changes and lability of emotion.

Chronic obstructive airways disease (COAD), includes asthma, emphysema and chronic bronchitis. Episodes of shortness of breath in COAD set off a reaction of anxiety and depression which unfortunately make the breathing worse.

Cancer of the pancreas is sometimes preceded by depression as long as a year or two ahead of other symptoms. There is intractable insomnia, regardless of hypnotics, and a sense of impending doom. There is also deep abdominal or back pain.

Severe iron deficiency anaemia may produce memory deficits and episodes of confusion. Paranoid features are more likely in anaemia due to lack of vitamin B12 or folic acid. The symptoms of mild anaemia of either type are non-specific and vague: for example fatigue and poor concentration.

Epilepsy: between fits there are sometimes psychotic episodes, easily misdiagnosed as schizophrenia. These occur, typically, with a left-sided epileptic focus, while depression is more likely with a focus on the right.

Temporal lobe epilepsy is frequently associated with visual, olfactory or gustatory hallucinations. A slow-growing temporal lobe tumour may produce the same effects.

Finally, there is a particular risk of claims for *psychiatric negligence* when there are obvious psychiatric symptoms masking a physical disorder. Litigation is likely to follow the failure to make a full, meticulously-recorded assessment in such a case, followed by failure to diagnose the organic condition. The side-effects of any psychotropic drugs prescribed may compound the situation, particularly if the patient was not adequately forewarned.

CHAPTER SEVEN

POST-TRAUMATIC STRESS DISORDER

Post-traumatic stress disorder (PTSD) is currently a very popular diagnosis, frequently met with in compensation cases. Since it is often claimed on inadequate or incorrect grounds, it is essential to have full, accurate knowledge of the condition.

History

PTSD is basically a sustained reaction to extreme, usually life-threatening stress. It has only been recognised in its present form and under its present name since 1980, and only became the basis for compensation in 1989 through a case brought about by the disaster of *The Herald of Free Enterprise* ferry. Nevertheless, the symptom-complex of PTSD has been known for over 100 years under various other names. Among the earliest was 'spinal shock,' resulting from the alarming railway accidents of the last century. 'Battle fatigue' was the term applied to the stressed soldiers of the American Civil War, while 'psychasthenia' referred to the same condition in 1909.

In the First World War 'shell-shock' and disorderly action of the heart (DAH) were the diagnoses covering most cases of PTSD. At this stage the condition was seen as essentially physical, but it was noticed that some men suffered just as badly as the others after exposure to the trauma, despite having no actual wound. By 1940, in the Second World War, the military psychiatrists, Sargant and Slater, recognised 'battle shock' and 'battle neurosis' as psychiatric disorders, and demonstrated that they were susceptible to psychiatric treatment. In 1943 there was a devastating fire at the Coconut Grove night club in New York. People were trapped and terrified. It was found that half of them were still suffering from an anxiety neurosis three months later, and a quarter as long as nine months later. Crisis Theory and its corollary, Coping Theory, were popular terms in the post-war era, and the principle was established that prompt psychological support is important in the face of extreme stress. Today armies of counsellors move in whenever there is a disaster.

In the Korean and, even more, in the Vietnam War, many servicemen suffered persistent nervous symptoms, and, although the condition was not fully understood, the United States government paid compensation to many of its Veterans. The further knowledge of PTSD developed through a series of specific disasters such as the fire on the Piper Alpha oil rig, Lockerbie (where a terrorist bomb blew up an airliner), bush fires in Australia, and particular episodes in the Falklands War.

Prevalence

The life-time prevalence rate of PTSD in the developed countries is 1.3% and its incidence after a major disaster varies between 20% and 90%, depending on the circumstances.

Causes

The precipitating cause of PTSD is commonly a life-threatening disaster, unexpected and that which the victim or victims could not avoid. It is defined in ICD-10 as being of an exceptionally threatening or catastrophic nature, which is likely to cause pervasive distress in almost anyone.

Onlooker trauma: the situation of the helpless onlooker at a disaster is extremely stressful and should not be ignored.

Example: when an IRA bomb exploded in the concourse of Victoria Station at ground level, a number of people sustained serious injuries to the lower half of their bodies. There were many casualties going through the operating theatre at Westminster Hospital, including those requiring amputations. The surgeons and theatre sister were exhausted but unscathed psychologically, but the junior nurses, who were only standing by, watching the surgery but with little else to do, were affected for many weeks afterwards. Some developed the full PTSD syndrome.

Predisposing causes

- age: both children and the elderly are especially vulnerable;
- personal or family history of psychiatric disorder;
- sensitive, introverted personality;
- previous upsetting life experience, for instance sexual abuse in childhood;
- there is some evidence of a genetic disposition to react to psychological trauma with PTSD.

The likelihood of PTSD increases with the severity of the stress. Some 80% of Cambodian refugees from torture, war and loss, seeking asylum in the United States, still had the symptoms of PTSD a year later, while only 20% of British soldiers in the Falklands War developed stress symptoms.

Any psychological shock produces an emotional reaction, and this is regarded as normal if it amounts to no more than an 'acute reaction to stress' or a brief 'adjustment reaction'. The first is characteristically transient, arising within minutes of the event and subsiding within hours, or, at most, two or three days. The victim at first feels dazed and then becomes anxious and restless. A brief adjustment reaction develops within a month of a stressful event or a change and lasts no more than a month. Its manifestations vary, but include a low mood, anxiety or worry, and a feeling of being unable to cope.

Either of these conditions, if short-lived as described, are not regarded as worthy of compensation. For this, the patient must have suffered appreciable psychological damage, manifest in:

- persistence of the acute stress or adjustment reaction over months, when it is regarded as a definite disorder;
- a prolonged anxiety state, with or without panic attacks or phobias;
- personality change, perhaps with unaccustomed anti-social behaviour;
- psychosis, for instance schizophrenic (rare);
- PTSD.

The other necessary condition for a successful claim for compensation is the demonstration of a breach of duty by someone or some body which has led directly to the patient's injury or illness.

Those of any age can be affected by PTSD, including children. The symptoms may begin immediately after the stressful event, after a few days, or occasionally, after a few months. PTSD is considered acute when the symptoms last less than three months, chronic when they continue for three months or more, and delayed when they do not appear for six months or more after the event. Sometimes the symptoms are triggered by a second trauma, which may be a relatively minor occurrence.

Case

J was an arts student of 19 when he was involved in the King's Cross escalator fire. At first it looked as though he and some others would be trapped underground, but in fact J reached safety unscathed except for minor scratches and burns. These soon healed, and, except for a few disturbed nights at the beginning, he suffered no adverse psychological after-effects. He saw a counsellor twice but felt it was a waste of time, so gave it up.

It was eight months later, when J was travelling by tube to Oxford Circus, that there was a power failure, causing the train to stop in a tunnel. The carriage became increasingly hot and stuffy and J became increasingly anxious. It was nearly two hours later that the train left for the next station. Within two days J had developed the typical symptoms of PTSD.

The characteristics of PTSD

These fall into three groups:

1 Arousal symptoms
   - persistent anxiety;
   - irritability;

- startle response;
- insomnia, usually initial and middle;
- inability to concentrate.

2   Intrusions
- intense, intrusive re-living of the trauma (flashbacks);
- difficulty in recalling the stressful events at will;
- recurrent distressing nightmares, usually connected with the trauma.

3   Avoidance
- numbing of the emotions;
- loss of interest in normal activities;
- avoidance of the place or other reminders of the event.

Depressive symptoms are also common, often accompanied by survivor guilt – guilt because some other people had a worse outcome.

A number of those exposed to a terrifying ordeal develop several of the symptoms of PTSD. The criteria in DSM-IV are precise and exacting, however, and it is important to know them. They comprise:

A   Exposure to a traumatic event in which both of the following were present:
- actual or threatened death or serious injury to self or others;
- response involving intense fear, helplessness or horror (children may show disorganised behaviour).

B   The event is persistently re-experienced in one or more of these ways:
- recurrent, intrusive recollections or images of the traumatic event (children may play it out);
- recurrent distressing dreams of the event (children may have non-specific nightmares);
- acting or feeling as though the event were recurring, with illusions or hallucinations (children may act the event);
- intense distress is reaction to any reminder, including symbolic, of the event;
- physiological reactions to such reminders (sweating, tremor, palpitations, pallor).

C   Persistent avoidance of stimuli associated with the trauma, numbing of responsiveness, shown by three or more of the following:
- efforts to avoid thoughts, feelings or talk about the trauma;
- efforts to avoid anything that is a reminder of the trauma;
- inability to recall some important aspect of the trauma;
- much diminished interest or participation in usual activities;
- feeling of detachment from others;

- unable to have normal emotions, eg loving feelings;
- inability to see any future for self.

D Persistent symptoms of arousal, shown by two or more of the following:

- difficulty falling or staying asleep;
- irritability or outbursts of anger;
- poor concentration;
- exaggerated startled response to noise;
- over-alertness.

E Symptoms in B, C and D continuing for more than a month.

F Clinically significant distress, or impaired social, occupational or other important area of functioning.

Case

AG was 23, with an apparently useless degree in anthropology: he had been looking for work, suitable or otherwise, for over a year and had found only temporary fill-ins. He was in despair when the Job Centre found him a place as a trainee in a well-known advertising firm. The job itself comprised a boring clerical routine, but the venue was impressive. It was a large Victorian building in the process of major refurbishment, currently concentrated in the area immediately above the area in which AG worked, or so it seemed from the noise being created.

It was one lunchtime, when AG happened to be in the office alone, catching up on some work, that it happened. There was a rending sound and a great chunk of Victorian ceiling landed on his desk, glancing off his shoulder as it fell, followed by a shower of lesser fragments. AG felt that he was about to be crushed by the whole building collapsing around him, but nothing happened. The workmen were off on their lunchbreak but AG's colleagues came back when they heard the racket, and took him to the local hospital's accident and emergency department. AG was scratched and bruised but had suffered no serious injury. He was given a collar to wear for a few days and some analgesics, and told to rest for a day or two.

At first AG merely felt numb, but on the third day, when he was expected to go back to work, he became increasingly anxious, 'jumping' at the slightest noise and snapping at anyone who spoke to him. He also started having nightmares, some, but not all, about the accident. This continued for two or three weeks, then gradually ceased. He found he was thinking about the accident several times a day. His anxiety subsided but a more depressive mood took over. Meanwhile AG's job was kept open, but he kept putting off his return to work. In the end one of the girls he worked with suggested he should go back with her and just 'get the feel' of the place: the ceiling was perfectly secure now. The visit to the office was not a success and merely confirmed AG's feeling that he could not go back.

At this stage his father encouraged him to bring a case for compensation against his employer. As his physical injuries were slight and had anyway long since recovered, the basis of the claim was post-traumatic stress disorder which was preventing him from working and living a normal life. The diagnosis was crucial to his case and the legal argument ranged around the precise criteria for PSTD, and whether AG's symptoms conformed to them.

Category A: it was suggested by the defence that the ceiling's partial collapse was insufficient to make AG believe that he was in danger of death or serious injury, but the latter seemed plausible.

Category B: although AG had distressing dreams, these had only continued for two or three weeks and were not all about the accident, specifically, but he did keep thinking about it for far longer. On balance there seemed to be enough to comply with this category.

Category C: AG certainly showed two of the three necessary items: efforts to avoid his workplace, and diminished interest and participation in a significant activity, ie work.

Category D: AG had continuing difficulty in concentrating and still 'jumped' at any sudden noise, according with this category.

Category E: most of AG's symptoms lasted for more than a month, but not the nightmares, nor the anxiety state.

Category F: AG's symptoms conformed fully.

In the event, it was decided that a diagnosis of PTSD was reasonable and AG received compensation accordingly.

PTSD in children

Children are by no means immune to the disorder, but there is no special paediatric category for PTSD in either DSM-IV or ICD-10. While children often present the same basic picture as adults, with disturbed sleep, nightmares and flashbacks, they may have other symptoms:

- irrational separation anxiety, unable to bear their mother to be out of sight, including at night;
- regressive behaviour such as thumb-sucking or bed-wetting and babyish talk.

Children who have been subject to physical or sexual abuse are especially vulnerable, but in any case the symptoms may last from six to 12 months.

Mechanisms producing PTSD

Neurophysiological theories suggest that PTSD involves classical conditioning: learning (to fear) at a subcortical level. The only measurable change after exposure to major trauma is an increase in noradrenergic activity in some cases: a response to perceived danger. Other theories are of a depletion of endorphins in the brain, or a blunting of cortico-adrenal responsivity. All of this is controversial.

Psychological theories suggest the reactivation by the trauma of early subconscious memories, or – from the cognitive school – that the trauma is so great that it overwhelms the brain's normal protective responses, allowing intrusive thoughts and images to leak through. None of these theories is helpful or particularly convincing and further research is needed.

Eligibility for compensation because of PTSD

Which people have a valid complaint? This question has been fought over in the courts in association with the Hillsborough disaster. Those judged fit to qualify for compensation include:

- anyone directly subjected to the serious trauma (eg involved in the car crash);
- an onlooker seeing a close relative killed;
- anyone seeing a close relative killed on live television;
- hearing about the disastrous death of a close relative from a third party, eg the police, shortly after the event.

Hearing about the disaster on the radio or a television recording later did not count as the exceptionally threatening experience required for a diagnosis of PTSD. Argument has also ranged around how close a close relative should be to qualify. It was originally limited to spouse, child or sibling, and a nephew, fiance or half-brother was excluded. This was later changed and now it lies with the plaintiff to show that there had been a strong bond of love and affection between him the person who was killed.

Case

McLoughlin: *McLoughlin v O'Brian* [1982] 2 WLR 982, 998. The plaintiff's husband and three children were involved in a road traffic accident in which one of the children was killed. The plaintiff was not with them, but was taken to the hospital soon afterwards. There she was told of the death of her child and allowed to see the other members of the family who were severely injured. This was about two hours after the accident. Mrs McLoughlin's claim for compensation for post-traumatic psychiatric illness caused by these events was upheld in the House of Lords, but points to consider in assessing similar claims were outlined:

- closeness of the emotional tie between the plaintiff and the primary victim?
- if the plaintiff did not actually witness the event were they involved in the immediate aftermath naturally as being spouse or parent of the victim?
- was the plaintiff's psychiatric illness caused by the sight of or hearing of the event or its immediate aftermath?

It was ruled that the immediate aftermath would not include seeing the body of a loved one in a mortuary eight or nine hours later. Mrs McLoughlin's two-hour delay was at the limit.

Circumstances of traumatic shock consistent with the development of PTSD

- some active service situations;
- natural disasters such as earthquakes, volcanoes, hurricanes or forest fires;
- terrorist attacks;
- rape;
- personal assault;
- torture previously experienced by asylum seekers: these people are likely to suffer years of PTSD.

Treatment of PTSD

This comprises immediate care after the traumatic event and treatment of established PTSD.

Immediate measures: these include sympathetic companionship, usually from a counsellor, with encouragement to talk about what happened and the emotions aroused. The patient's experiences should be rehearsed over and over again until they lose their sharpest impact. When several people have been injured and emotionally traumatised, they benefit from being kept together so that they can share their feelings and give each other informed support. A few doses of an anxiolytic, especially at night, may be helpful, but should only be given for the first few days.

Although counselling and 'working through' the distress is considered the best form of management, there is no convincing evidence that it accelerates recovery, but as yet there is nothing else as cheap and easily available.

Later treatment: supportive psychotherapy from a psychiatrist or clinical psychologist, rather than simple counselling, may be necessary, or cognitive behavioural therapy aimed at desensitising the patient to intrusive thoughts and fears. This method helps some patients but can make the symptoms worse for a few.

Drug treatment: benzodiazepine anxiolytics should be avoided in these vulnerable, established patients. They easily become dependent. Antidepressants, such as fluoxetine or some of the tricyclics are sometimes beneficial.

Prognosis

This is difficult to judge and is largely dependent on the patient's personal circumstances: family, job, partner, finances. However, while one-quarter of PTSD sufferers are symptom-free within three months, and one-half within six months, as many as 46% will continue to have some of the symptoms for several years, regardless of treatment. Litigation is sometimes suspected of prolonging the disorder, but there is no statistical evidence of this. Most victims improve after a settlement is made, whether or not they have been involved in litigation.

Planning for disaster

Local authorities and those in charge of large establishments, whether or not fraught with risks, such as coal mines or nuclear power stations, or apparently safe, such as infant schools or offices, have a responsibility to be prepared for major, unpredicted disasters. There should be rapid response arrangements in place, including those for psychological injury. The latter includes having counsellors available when needed. This means recruiting and training volunteers who are willing to be called upon at short notice. Training of professionals and other staff is also vital, so that in a crisis each person already knows what to do.

A case for negligence could be brought if employers and others in authority fail to make adequate arrangements for what may have seemed unlikely ever to happen. As described with the Victoria Station bomb, the hospital staff who had a definite task did not suffer the psychological trauma of those who did not know what to do.

CHAPTER EIGHT

DEPRESSION

Depression is common, widespread and as old as history itself. The ancient Greeks called it melancholia and put it down to an excess of black bile, and in 17th century England the cleric, Robert Burton, wrote his Anatomy of Melancholy, based on his own experience. Since it causes so much suffering and impairment of function at work and at home, the Royal College of Psychiatrists has been running a year-long campaign: Defeat Depression. This has stimulated public and professional awareness and increased the likelihood of depression figuring in litigation.

There is no one who has not, at some time, felt sad, miserable or even despairing. This is a normal response to adversity.

Case

Mr W had had trouble with his flat roof for years. In the end, at great expense, he replaced it with a new one made of the latest materials. At the first heavy burst of rain it leaked in all the old places. Mr W said he was in despair: understandable in the circumstances. He was able to sue the roofers for their bad workmanship, but not for causing him psychological damage.

Most lay people and some lawyers would have said that Mr W was depressed, but his reaction was a normal one, not the pathological state that comprises a clinical depressive illness. It is the latter which is likely to concern the medico-legal practitioner. It can be distinguished from ordinary unhappiness because the sadness is more severe, has a special pervasive quality, and lasts for weeks, at least; it is accompanied by other features of the depressive syndrome.

Epidemiology

Today, in the industrialised world, there is a 17% life-time risk of having a depressive illness. Women are affected twice as often as men, although some depressed men may double as alcoholics. No age is exempt, from early childhood to the senium. Contrary to popular belief, the likelihood of depression does not increase with the years: the highest proportion of depressives is in the age group 18–24. Exceptions are those in the depressive phase of a manic depressive illness: this affects men as often as women, and the onset is often in late adolescence or early adulthood, or in those over the age of 60.

Clinical picture of depressive illness

The most striking feature is a general depression of vitality. The mood is low and hopeless and nothing seems worthwhile. All activity and, most obviously, self-care, is reduced: the patient may sit about, unshaven or without make-up, staring at nothing. Everything is an effort and he readily gives up. There is a general slowing down of speech, thinking and movement. Concentration is poor and the patient finds himself reading the same paragraph over and over again. In a significant minority of patients, usually the middle-aged and older patients, instead of retardation there is agitation: speech, thought and body are in a constant, restless ferment but nothing is achieved. The fingers twist and fidget.

Judgment is seriously impaired in depression because the victim sees past, present and future as equally black: the past laden with regrets, the present with things to fear, and the future, if any, a matter of dread. Every action seems pointless so decision-making is neglected. The low mood is often accompanied by an unrealistic conviction of guilt, especially in Judao-Christian societies. This is of a different character from the ordinary tendency to blame oneself for letting people down by being ill. Ruminations of worthlessness, abject poverty or contagion with evil may preoccupy the patient's thoughts, and sometimes reach delusional force. Before the advent of anti-depressants, severely ill patients could slip into a depressive stupor: this is not seen nowadays.

Case: Lady J, aged 44, was significantly wealthy. During her depressive illness she was overcome with shame because she believed that all she possessed in the world was one pair of knickers, and that all her relatives had died. The latter visited her and her bank manger did his best to reassure her, but to no avail until the anti-depressants had achieved their slow effect.

Adolescents and young adults often present with a angry, irritable mood and their underlying depression may be missed. Another trap with this age group is the possibility of incipient schizophrenia presenting with depression, especially when there are hallucinations or delusions, as may occur in severe, psychotic depression. The hallucinations are usually auditory, consisting of voices making denigratory or derisory comments about the patient. Rarely, there are visual hallucinations of death scenes.

Biological symptoms

- Loss of appetite, with weight loss of 5% or more in a month; alternatively, but less often the patient over-eats, without enjoyment, and gains weight.
- Sleep disturbance, usually consisting of waking, bleakly alert, late at night and in the very early morning; occasionally patients suffer hypersomnia instead.

- Constipation results from the body's general slow-down and the lack of residue.
- The blink rate is often abnormally slow, making the patient appear to stare.
- Diurnal variation of mood: the early morning is the worst time, but the mood may lighten slightly during the day. For some patients the pattern is reversed, with the most severe depression in the evening.
- Some patients spend much of the 24 hours in bed, too wretched to sleep.

Case

RL, an unmarried woman of 52, living with a widowed mother, was told that she must take compulsory early retirement from the clerical post at the University. She had been there for 29 years. RL went home and crawled under the bedclothes, fully dressed, and shut her eyes, but she did not sleep. She spent most of the next five weeks in bed, living on bowls of cornflakes. This was a regression to infancy and an indication of the profound sense of helplessness that affects some depressives.

MAJOR DEPRESSIVE DISORDER

This is the term favoured by DSM-IV and ICD-10 for a serious clinical depression. Neither classification is particularly convenient, but it is useful to have an approved checklist for the main illness:

First, there must have been a distinct difference from normal in the patient's mood and functioning for at least two weeks, with a loss of interest in his usual activities. Others may notice the change before the patient reports it himself.

Secondly, he must show at least four of the following symptoms:
- loss of appetite and weight, or increased intake and weight gain;
- retardation or agitation;
- lack of energy, fatigue;
- insomnia, or hypersomnia;
- morbid thoughts or suicidal ideas;
- feelings of worthlessness or inappropriate guilt;
- poor concentration and indecisiveness.

There are numerous subgroups of major depressive disorder, but neither DSM-IV nor ICD-10 is particularly helpful in classifying them. The two most important are:

Unipolar depression, which may or may not be recurrent,

Bipolar depression, which alternates with episodes of mania.

Recurrent unipolar and bipolar types are more likely to be of psychotic intensity, and, importantly, they have a major genetic component in their aetiology. This makes it more difficult to argue that they have been caused by a trauma for which some other person or institution can be held responsible.

Other types include:

Seasonal affective disorder (SAD) which tends to come on every year in the autumn, when there is less daylight, but it is more likely when there are other demands on the patient.

Mixed affective disorder which is a combination of depressive and hypomanic symptoms, so that the patient's mood keeps changing.

Bereavement is a normal reaction to serious loss, usually of a person, but it can be of a career or home. It is characterised by a period of numbness, followed by waves of sadness, tearfulness and inability to concentrate, loss of appetite and weight loss, insomnia, guilt – however inappropriate – towards the person who has died, and sometimes hallucinations associated with them. Bereavement may be complicated by a major depressive disorder, manifest in additional symptoms of retardation, preoccupation with suicidal ideas, inability to cope, a feeling of uselessness and, in some cases, delusions.

Milder depressive disorders

Dysthymic disorder or neurotic depression often continues for two years or more, fluctuating in severity. It comprises many of the symptoms of major depressive disorder, but less severe, and without weight loss, suicidal thoughts, hallucinations or delusions.

Depression secondary to another psychiatric disorder, for instance schizophrenia, alcoholism, dementia and some types of personality disorder.

Depression as a drug side-effect

This may become a subject for litigation, especially if the patient does not feel he was forewarned about this possible side-effect. Drugs which may cause depression include:

- steroids, including oral contraceptives;
- beta-blockers;
- alpha-methyldopa;
- L-dopa;
- tetrabenazine;
- phenytoin;

- baclofen;
- cycloserine;
- isoniazid;
- co-trimoxazole;
- cycloserine;
- disulfiram;
- indomethacin.

Depression secondary to physical illness

See Chapter 6.

Legal cases involving the diagnosis of depression

Depression is the psychiatric diagnosis most likely to figure in court cases, particularly in:

- claims for compensation, including medical negligence, often but not invariably as a secondary factor when an injury has occurred.
- mitigation of a sentence: the offender's lawyer asks for his mental state at the time of the offence to be taken into consideration.

Case

Miss G had looked after an invalid mother for a number of years, her father having disappeared when she was a young child. Her mother had now died. With her 40th birthday looming ominously, Miss G felt that the outlook for future employment was uncertain, and this made her all the more anxious to cement her relationship with Ross. He was three years younger than her, and beginning to think seriously of settling down. He had hinted that one day he would want to have children: this was a problem for Miss G. Apart from her age, Miss G knew that she had almost no chance of conceiving having had several severe bouts of pelvic inflammatory disease. She had not told Ross and when he was sent on a six months' engineering contract to Saudi Arabia the temptation arose.

She wrote to Ross that she was three months pregnant, but had not liked to tell him until she was sure. As the time grew near for his return Miss G became desperate and seized the opportunity of snatching a tiny baby from his pram while his mother was buying groceries. Miss G was traced and arrested within 10 days. There was no doubt about her guilt, but her counsel hoped to show that that she had been suffering from a depressive illness in reaction to her mother's fairly recent death. Unfortunately she had not consulted her general practitioner so there was no record of her mental state at the time of the offence, but her lawyers arranged a psychiatric assessment as soon as they could.

Miss G was by then extremely anxious and showed some symptoms that could also have been due to depression: impaired sleep and concentration. These were not enough to fulfill the criteria for a major depressive disorder. She was anxious about the case rather than seriously depressed. She was by no means slowed down, she was eating more than usual as is common in anxiety, and although she felt guilty, this was not without cause. The evidence for depression was not convincing, but fortunately for Miss G there is a general belief that women who steal babies are behaving under the influence of strong emotion, and that psychiatric treatment is more appropriate than punishment.

Had Miss G been convicted of stealing an inanimate object of value, a firm diagnosis of depression would have been necessary to mitigate her sentence.

There is another situation which arises from time to time, when the offender's likely depressive state of mind is taken into consideration: the so-called mercy killing of a relative who is dying in pain and distress. In these cases the offender has been in such an unbearable position that depression is seen as almost inevitable.

Claims for compensation because of depression occur frequently.

Case

Ms Z had an intrauterine contraceptive device (IUCD) fitted after her second termination. She did not like the idea of taking the contraceptive pill every day, and for one reason or another she found the barrier and chemical methods unreliable. However, the relationship with her Irish boyfriend developed and they decided to have a baby together, and then, perhaps, to marry. Ms Z asked the gynaecologist to remove the IUCD at the same time as she underwent a minor procedure to the cervix, and she was told that this had been done. To her surprise and disappointment Ms Z did not immediately conceive.

Some six years later, after numerous fruitless infertility investigations, she and her boyfriend split up. He formed a relationship with another woman who quickly became pregnant and bore him a son. Deeply upset Ms Z moved out of London where she fell under a different hospital and Health Authority. When she saw the gynaecologist at the new hospital because of pelvic pain, he arranged a plain X-ray. The IUCD was plainly visible *in situ*: it had never been removed. Miss Z had naturally been unhappy before this revelation, but the realisation that she had wasted years believing that she was infertile, finally losing her partner over it, unnecessarily, precipitated her into a severe depressive illness. There was no doubt about the diagnosis. She was unable to carry on with her work at the bakery, involving a loss of income lasting nearly a year.

The negligence of the original gynaecologist was undeniable and Ms Z was paid a substantial sum for suffering a depressive illness, and damage to her life, although physically she was unharmed. Many cases involve a procedure that goes wrong, leaving the patient with scarring at best, or some loss of function, such as incontinence of urine, complicated by depression.

The new offence of stalking is interesting because although that causes no physical damage, it has been judged to be responsible for grievous bodily harm: the concept being stretched to accommodate psychological injury, for instance depressive illness.

CAUSES OF MAJOR DEPRESSIVE DISORDER

These are important when there is a need to apportion blame for the development of the illness.

Genetic: the relatives of severely depressed patients stand nearly three times the risk of the population in general of suffering from the illness themselves. This means that only a small amount of stress is needed to trigger a depression in these cases. In the minority type bipolar depression, the genetic link is even more potent, and the illness may appear without any appreciable precipitant.

Personality: obsessionals, perfectionists and those prone to worry are types most vulnerable to depression.

Early environment: deprivation of maternal affection, through separation or death, has been shown to predispose to depression in adult life. The effects of parental discord in the run-up to divorce, followed by virtual separation from one parent, is equally damaging.

Predisposing life-events: it often seems that the event that precipitates a depressive episode is 'the last straw' after a period of losses or difficulties at home or at work. With an unhappy marriage and an ever-present fear of redundancy, a comparatively small adverse event may trigger a full-scale depression. A trivial medical error, producing, for example, an almost invisible scar in an inaccessible place, may be sufficient to set off a genuine depression in such circumstances.

Precipitating factors: these are of crucial importance in medico-legal practice. It is a matter of everyday clinical observation that depressive disorders frequently follow a traumatic experience or event and may reasonably be attributed to it. This can form the basis of a claim for compensation.

Biochemical markers: it would be convenient if neuroendocrine tests could be used in the diagnosis of depression. Unfortunately they are both expensive and inconsistent, including the dexamethasone suppression test which is positive in only 50% of severely depressed patients.

SUICIDE AND SELF-HARM

Official suicide rates in the United Kingdom account for 1% of all deaths, but this is certainly an underestimate, partly because of the strict rule that an open verdict or one of accidental death must be returned in the absence of definite evidence for suicide. The rate for young males has been rising over recent years, but is falling for women. There are three male suicides to one female in the United Kingdom and in France and Germany.

Associations

1　Psychiatric disorder (nine out of ten), especially depression and alcoholism.
2　Male sex.
3　Spring and summer: March is the peak month.
4　Divorce (widows and widowers are the next most vulnerable).
5　Professional classes and the unskilled.
6　Veterinary surgeons, doctors, pharmacists and farmers (access to drugs).
7　Social isolation.
8　Physical illness in the elderly.
9　Prisoners on remand.
10　Copycats.
11　Chronic, painful, physical illness.
12　Prolonged unemployment plus poor physical health: especially women.

Assessment of risk: a doctor's duty

This requires attention to the risk factors, and what the patient says. Most suicides have told someone, often their doctor, of their intent within days of the deed. It does not make suicide more likely to inquire specifically about thoughts of suicide.

A high index of suspicion should be aroused with:
- previous suicide attempts;
- depressive illness with anorexia, weight loss, insomnia and hopelessness.

Deliberate self-harm

In 90% of cases of deliberate self-harm in the United Kingdom the method is drug overdosage. It can be construed as negligent to prescribe to depressives unsafe quantities of drugs which could harm them, for instance the cardiotoxic tricyclics, particularly since many of these patients do not want to die, but simply want to make a statement. Paracetamol, available over the counter, has caused many deaths because of its effects being more dangerous than the patients had expected.

Self-injury accounts for about 10% of all deliberate self-harm in Britain. The commonest type is wrist-cutting, which is used by certain personalities for relief of tension. Serious mutilation, for instance amputating the penis, usually occurs in deluded schizophrenics, fortunately rarely. Medical negligence is not likely to be involved since it is usually impossible to anticipate these acts.

CHAPTER NINE

LOSS OF MEMORY

Memory disorder is of the utmost significance in medico-legal psychiatric practice. It is one of the most sensitive indicators of brain damage or dysfunction, and often the deciding factor in the diagnosis of cerebral disease. Yet it also occurs, or appears to occur, when there is no such disease.

Most of us, as children, 'forgot' some action or event – for instance how a broken vase turned up behind the sofa – when to remember would have been tantamount to admitting to a crime. Similarly, it is not unusual for an adult who is accused of some criminal offence to claim that he cannot remember what happened at the crucial time. In fact this occurs in 10% of prisoners on remand and in 40% of cases of homicide. However, this loss of memory is unlikely to help matters.

The law

Inability to recall an offence and the circumstances surrounding it is no defence in law. Nevertheless, a severe impairment of memory, for instance after a head injury, may raise questions about fitness to plead. A serious psychiatric disorder, involving, *inter alia*, memory loss, may be considered in mitigation of a sentence. The concept of diminished responsibility, because of the mental state is often used to reduce a charge of murder to one of manslaughter. It is essential to make a detailed psychiatric assessment whenever an accused person shows even a small degree of amnesia.

Memory is of vital importance in many civil cases. Usually it is a simple matter of difficulty in remembering the details after the event as there is often an unconscionably long time before the plaintiff in a compensation case consults her solicitor, let alone goes to court. Road Traffic Accidents are notorious for the difference in the accounts given by participants and witnesses. Added to this, there may be a psychiatric cause for impaired memory.

HOW MEMORY WORKS

Memory is a complex of functions for dealing with information coming in through the senses. Various types of information are processed differently, according to the uses to which they will be put. A telephone number may need to be retained for a matter of seconds only, but it is convenient if you manage to remember the date of your wedding anniversary indefinitely! Memory is made up of four functions:

- registration;
- retention;
- recognition;
- retrieval or recall.

Registration depends on attention and concentration, which can be distracted by external factors such as noise, and disturbed by a variety of psychiatric disorders.

Retention is the essence of memory, and in itself consists of several parts:

- immediate, sensory memory lasting less than a second;
- primary memory (also called short-term memory by psychologists): information is held for 15–20 seconds, but may be retained for longer by repetition, for instance of someone's name when you are introduced. Visual and verbal impressions are recorded separately. The primary memory is also called the 'working memory' since it is used for holding the information you need for the task in hand, eg knitting a scarf or working out a bill;
- secondary or long-term memory: this stores material selected for more enduring retention. Clinicians divide it into two types, confusingly referred to as *long-term* or remote memory, and *short-term* or recent memory. The first comprises long past memories, those retained and enjoyed by the old. The second type is applicable to recent events, from minutes to weeks ago. It is recent memory that is the give-away, the most obviously impaired when there is a general intellectual short-fall, as in Alzheimer's disease. It is selectively impaired in the fascinating amnestic syndrome, described later in this chapter.

Recognition is the mental process by which an item in the memory is recognised as relevant to the current task, for instance answering an examination question. Recognition is also used in its more familiar way, to mean the instant identification of a person or piece of knowledge presented to you.

Retrieval or recall is the bringing of a memory to conscious awareness, with or without a cue. This is the crunch point, and even when you know someone's name perfectly well, you can have difficulty in calling it to mind at will. This is normal.

MEMORY TESTING

In ordinary clinical practice the patient's ability to register, retain and retrieve information can be assessed by a few simple tests. One simple ploy is to ask the patient to repeat a sentence immediately after hearing it. For example, an average adult should be able to repeat: 'The redheaded woodpeckers made a terrible fuss as they tried to drive the young away from the nest.' Or a name and address may be given and when it is repeated accurately the patient is asked to repeat it again five minutes later.

Questions to ask

- remote personal events, such as year of birth, name of school, first job;
- recent personal events, such as menu at last meal, names and roles of people seen today, last night's television;
- general events, such as an item of news, name of the Prime Minister, dates of the two World Wars.

Special attention should be given to memory for recent events, and in particular for their sequence in time. Formal psychometric testing requires the particular skills of the psychologists. They use a whole battery of tests including the Williams and the Wechsler Memory Scales, and the Synonym Learning and Paired Associates Learning Tests respectively, among others. Properly presented, these detailed tests go a long way towards distinguishing organic from functional brain problems, sometimes pinpointing the area affected.

AMNESIA (LOSS OF MEMORY)

The two groups are:
1 Organic.
2 Psychogenic.

Organic group

Acute organic psychoses
These often come on in the course of a physical illness, after head injury or post-operatively.

They are characterised by:
- fluctuating consciousness and confusion, worse in the evening;
- disorientation in time, place and person, *disrupted memory*;
- visual illusions and hallucinations;
- intrusive, compelling fantasies;
- slow, muddled thinking;

- agitation and restlessness and fear;
- suspicion, misinterpretation and paranoia.

Not all of these symptoms are present and they vary in intensity from hour to hour: their onset is usually sudden, but in a physically sick patient may not be recognised straightaway.

Causes

Infection: meningitis, encephalitis, eg chicken pox, septicaemia, influenza, cerebral malaria.

In the elderly, urinary and respiratory infections may, unrecognised, lead to the syndrome, as may a small area of gangrene on the foot in a diabetic.

Head injury: acute traumatic psychosis for instance as happened to a 50 year old man who was walking past some scaffolding when a brick fell on his head. A subdural haematoma may result from a head injury.

Vascular: stroke, transient ischaemic attack, subarachnoid haemorrhage, hypertensive encephalopathy.

Epileptic: psychomotor fits, post-ictal states.

Tumours: primary or secondary.

Anoxia: pneumonia, silent coronary attack, congestive heart failure, post-anaesthetic, carbon monoxide poisoning.

Endocrine: hyperthyroid crisis, Addisonian crisis, myxoedema madness, hypoglycaemia.

Metabolic: uraemia, liver disorder, remote effects of cancer, electrolyte disturbances.

Vitamin deficiency: thiamine (Wernicke's encephalopathy), nicotinic acid, folic acid lack.

Toxic: alcohol, barbiturates (including withdrawal), cannabis, LSD, tricyclic and MAOI anti-depressants, anti-parkinsonian drugs, salicylates.

Anoxia, uraemia and liver disorder in particular may produce a subacute state in the elderly: this can be mistaken for dementia. On the other hand, an acute organic psychosis may usher in an incipient dementia. It is prudent to enquire about any previous problem with failing memory. In any event, to avoid an accusation of negligence investigations in all these acute organic states should include urinalysis, haematology, ESR, chest X-ray, blood urea, thyroid and liver function tests, blood sugar, and serum B12 and folate, EEG. Lumbar puncture may be necessary if the diagnosis remains in doubt.

Chronic organic psychoses

Causes

These include many of those for acute organic states, but also, in particular, the degenerative conditions.

Degenerative: Alzheimer's and Pick's diseases, multi-infarct dementia, Creuzfeldt-Jacob disease (CJD), Parkinson's disease, Huntington's chorea.

Trauma: post-traumatic dementia, particularly from the repeated trauma of boxing.

Toxic: alcoholic dementia, Korsakoff's syndrome.

Anoxia: anaemia, congestive heart failure, chronic respiratory disease, post-coronary, post-anaesthetic.

Vitamin deficiency: thiamine, nicotinic acid, B12, folic acid: in the elderly and those on their own, check the diet.

Metabolic and endocrine: as for acute states, but myxoedema, diabetes, liver and kidney failure, and cancers are more likely in older, chronic cases.

Clinical picture

- clear consciousness;
- progressive loss of memory;
- general fall-off in intellect and personality;
- reduction in self-care;
- shrinkage of vocabulary, less spontaneous speech;
- disorientation in time, place and person.

Korsakoff's psychosis

This is also called the amnestic syndrome. Symptoms are a drastic loss of short-term memory, dating from when the illness began (often with an acute organic psychosis due to a shortage of thiamine: Wernicke's encephalopathy), but a perfectly good memory for everything before that, and unimpaired intelligence. Patients are also able to register information for a second or two, and can repeat a name or a series of numbers immediately, but not five minutes later. Confabulation occurs when the patient fills in the gaps in memory in conversation by bringing in bits from past memories.

Case

Mr W, 56, was an expert in Chinese porcelain and advised museums and private collectors. His social manner was charming and his memory for items of porcelain prodigious. He had been a heavy social drinker for many years, but the damage it had caused to his brain was not recognised for a long time. When he was chatting with a friend about his collection, Mr W was asked, conversationally, how he had spent the morning. He said that he had been visiting the Queen in Buckingham Palace to see a vase, and described the rooms in accurate detail. But the Queen was on a tour of Canada. Mr W had indeed been called by her to give his opinion on a vase but five years previously.

Mr W's friend told a medical colleague of this curious conversation, and the result was that Mr W had a psychiatric examination, and was persuaded to give a Power of Attorney to his solicitor, since he was getting into a hopeless muddle with unpaid bills among other matters that he kept forgetting. His wife had left him some years before, because of the drinking. Mr W was given intensive treatment with thiamine, but did not improve enough to be able to manage his own affairs.

Sometimes a patient may have unrecognised Korsakoff's syndrome for a number of years. In that case, when he is examined he will not only have an appalling short-term memory, but he will appear to have a defective long-term memory as well: he may then be considered to be, and treated as though he were, demented.

Causes of the Korsakoff syndrome

Thiamine deficiency, due to:
- alcoholism (nearly always);
- carcinoma of the stomach;
- pregnancy;
- malabsorption;
- gross dietary deficiency;
- tumour;
- subarachnoid haemorrhage;
- carbon monoxide poisoning.

HEAD INJURY

If there is loss of consciousness with a head injury there is always some memory defect. This is of two types:

1 Retrograde: the time between the moment of injury and the last clear recollection before that. It usually spans a matter of minutes, and if it covers a longer period this is likely to be due partly to an emotional response to the injury.

2 Anterograde: if this lasts less than one hour, the outlook for intellectual and emotional recovery is good, but if it continues for more than a week lasting disability is likely.

Neurotic symptoms which may follow head injury:

- post-traumatic stress disorder;
- chronic anxiety, often fear of insanity;
- depression;
- headache: if persistent the possibility of a subdural haematoma should be remembered;
- post-concussional syndrome with irritability, dizziness, headache, fatigue, insomnia and ongoing poor memory.

Psychiatric disability after head injury is more likely if:

- injury was mild;
- there was little or no amnesia;
- previous personal or family history of psychiatric disorder;
- neurotic premorbid personality: especially vulnerable to changes in personality.

FUNCTIONAL PSYCHOSES CAUSING MEMORY IMPAIRMENT

Major depressive disorder

The common complaint of memory failure is usually due to failure to register what is going on because of lack of interest and attention. If the patient can be persuaded to concentrate his memory is found to be satisfactory.

Depressive pseudodementia can be deceptive since the slowing down and lack of self-care shown by depressives can be mistaken for brain failure, and they, too, frequently complain of poor memory.

A notorious case was that of Ernest Saunders, a director of the Guinness company, in his early seventies. He was jailed for alleged fraud (this is now being disputed). While he was in prison he developed symptoms, including loss of memory, which convinced two psychiatrists that he was suffering from Alzheimer's disease, which is inexorably progressive. Because of this illness he was released, but some months later he had apparently recovered. Clearly, he had not had Alzheimer's disease but a depressive illness with pseudodementia.

The reports did not mention whether Mr Saunders, when he appeared to be demented, was properly orientated for time and place. Usually, this is a good discriminator: depressives are correctly orientated, demented patients are not.

Of course, there can be co-existing depression and dementia: patients are often depressed in the early stages of Alzheimer's disease, when they are well enough in touch to be aware of their mental powers slipping away.

Mania, hypomania: a patient suffering from the manic stage of a manic-depressive illness does not complain of poor memory, although, during the acute phase, he is registering very little of what goes on. He is too distractible, turning his attention kaleidoscopically to anything that catches his eye or ear, and too involved in exciting, abnormal ideas, for example being the President of the World Bank rather than the manager of an unremarkable high street bank. He will not, of course, co-operate with any memory tests at this point. When the mania has subsided the patient will have only the haziest notion of his actions during the acute stage. This may be a mercy.

Case

Mr J-H, a pillar of boring respectability, had his first manic episode at 53. It might have mattered less if he had not been a bank manager. As it was he caused mayhem by merging his clients' accounts and using large sums to experiment in the futures market over a period of three days. He then startled everyone by removing all his clothes and his escapade came to a swift end. When he surfaced from the acute psychotic state he had no memory of what he had been doing, and was surprised to find that the bank wished him to retire at once, on medical grounds. It was not that Mr J-H did not remember what he had done that saved him from prosecution, but the incontrovertible evidence that he did not know what he was doing because of his mental state.

Schizophrenia

Acute schizophrenia resembles hypomania in that, during the illness, the registration of new information is impaired: the patient is preoccupied with his delusions and hallucinations. However, he does register – indelibly – any event or circumstance that chimes in emotionally with his abnormal thoughts and beliefs. As the acute phase of the psychosis settles, the patient's memory for it is poor and patchy, mixed with the delusional material which is now losing its force. The patient is not usually worried by this.

Chronic schizophrenia: long-standing patients, with the negative symptoms of poverty of thought, withdrawal and apathy, often show an uneven deterioration of memory both for past personal events, news and general information. This resembles the memory impairment of early dementia. Testing is difficult and unreliable in the presence of thought disorder, but as far as memory is concerned, the picture is basically that of an organic state.

NEUROTIC DISORDERS

In anxiety states, reactive depression and obsessive-compulsive neurosis, the patients' thoughts and concerns are bound up with themselves. They often complain of poor memory and may interpret it as the onset of Alzheimer's disease or of 'going mad'. Neurotics are often absent-minded, or too worried to concentrate on what they are doing: they mislay their keys, forget appointments, or omit vital items from the shopping list.

A particular type of memory loss occurs when a painful memory, or one that was laid down in harrowing circumstances, is suppressed through an unconscious mechanism. It is one of the criteria for post-traumatic stress disorder that there should be a partial loss of memory for the events surrounding the major disaster or personal trauma. Other psychological causes of suppression of particular memories may be associated with less dramatic, but emotionally charged, personal experiences.

Case

AA, a young woman presenting with chronic depression, was found to have a major gap in the memories of her childhood. This was found to be the time when her father had left the family. She had been his favourite, or so she believed, and the little girl – she was then aged six – could not accept his desertion. Full restoration of AA's memory for this period, and working through the feelings of hurt and disillusionment that belonged to that time, helped her to escape from her depression.

Childhood sexual abuse is a trauma which may be suppressed out of conscious memory. It is unfortunately no rarity, and is estimated as affecting 20–50% of children. Girls are involved more frequently than boys, at a ratio of 2–3:1. The child is usually afraid to speak about it at the time, because of threats of the dire consequences, the fear of not being believed, and a deep, unjustifiable sense of guilt. This situation increases the likelihood of suppression until some psychological upset, or a therapist brings the memory to light, often in early adulthood.

Long-term effects of childhood sexual abuse

- Long-term emotional disturbance, depression and anxiety manifest in 20% of victims, others develop psychosomatic disorders such as bulimia nervosa, while a few adopt the practise of self-mutilation. Feelings of worthlessness or worse and some of the symptoms of PTSD are common.
- Long-term disturbance of sexual behaviour. This ranges from avoidance of all sexual contact to gross promiscuity.

87

- Difficulty with interpersonal relationships because of ambivalent feelings and lack of trust.
- Tendency to drift into anti-social behaviour, for example prostitution, stealing, vandalism, and – in turn – the sexual abuse of young children in their care.

(See Cicchetti, D, Carlson, V (eds) (1989) in the section on Further Reading, p 127.)

Recovered memories

Psychotherapeutic techniques, including hypnosis, may be used to search for and restore lost memories. Recovering a memory enables it to be examined and dealt with in consciousness, hopefully with the relief of the neurotic symptoms. In the United States in particular there is a fashion for employing therapy to recover memories of being sexual abused in childhood, either within the family or in a children's 'home'. If normal memory does not oblige, recovered memories of early deprivation or abuse may be used in extenuation of anti-social or criminal acts in later life. So-called Survivors' Groups mull over the iniquities of their parents or carers, some claiming to remember details of abuse from the age of two. Families have been devastated by accusations of abusing their children in the past, and litigation against therapists is now commonplace in the United States.

Sigmund Freud, using his psychoanalytic techniques, was ahead of modern American psychiatry. He found that many of his female patients could be helped to recall sexual experiences in childhood involving a close relative, usually the father: this information he used in therapy. He then came to realise that many, if not most, of these patients were 'remembering' events that had not happened in reality, inadvertently encouraged by his interest.

False memories

Because of the spate of litigation occasioned by claims and counterclaims, insurers in the United States will no longer insure mental health therapists who employ hypnosis among other methods to assist their clients in recovering failed or repressed memories of possible abuse. The Canadian Psychiatric Association has stated that:

> ... if memories of events have not been revisited and cognitively rehearsed until ... some years later, it is not clear that such memories can be accessible, or can be reliable. Great caution should be exercised before acceptance in the absence of solid corroboration.

In recent cases in North America accusations of abuse based on recovered memories alone have all failed, and some unjustly accused fathers have been awarded damages.

False confessions

Confessions are usually made in the context of serious crime, especially murder, and a psychiatric opinion is sought if there is doubt about the validity of the statement. False confessions are of three types:

1 *Voluntary*: arising from an immature desire to be the centre of attention, to be important, in someone of no great attainments and of low self-esteem. The subject have difficulty in disentangling memory, fact and fantasy. There may be a compulsion to confess (and be forgiven) because of feelings of guilt unconnected with the particular offence, or confession may be made to protect someone else.

2 *Coerced-compliant*: this type of confession results from forceful interrogation, when the subject might agree to anything. It is this type which is most likely to be retracted later.

3 *Coerced-internalised*: these confessions occur when special interrogation techniques are used, or sometimes, inadvertently, as a result of psychotherapy. The person's genuine recollections are undermined and suggested 'memories' come to be believed.

Factors predisposing to false confession:

- head injury;
- recent bereavement;
- anxiety;
- guilt about other matters;
- immaturity: children, young people and those of limited intelligence are the most suggestible.

A psychiatrist or clinical psychologist may be asked to assess the subject's suggestibility, and hence the reliability of the confession.

In the cases in which the confession has been made for the sake of notoriety, the subject may be charged with wasting police time.

GLOBAL MEMORY LOSS

Dissociative fugue is a common presentation. Typically, the patient is found wandering somewhere well removed from his usual surroundings, with no knowledge of how he got there, nor of his personal identity. Such people are not usually distressed or even worried, since the dissociation is a subconscious mechanism for escaping from stress.

Sometimes it is because of a sexual indiscretion that the person dare not go home and explain; sometimes it is because of a devastating loss of self-esteem.

Case

A millionaire Israeli property dealer, Mr R, came to London to see his two sons and to demonstrate to them his expertise in the property market. His English was poor and his local knowledge grossly inadequate. He lost much of his fortune and was humiliated in the eyes of his sons. Mr R was found wandering by the river, with no idea of why he was there or who he was. It seems that his dissociative fugue had saved him from committing suicide. There is, however, an enhanced risk of suicide in these cases, when the person finally has to accept the reality of their situation. Mr R took an overdose, but his sons rushed him to hospital where he was kept in for psychiatric treatment.

Psychogenic amnesia does not include general knowledge, how to read, or operate a television set or a telephone. Reasoning powers are unimpaired and self-care is not neglected as would be the case with an organic loss of memory.

This could raise a suspicion that the patient is simulating his amnesia, especially if it emerges that he has been accused of some criminal offence. It is a pointer to deliberate deception if all clues to the person's identity – letters, credit card, season ticket etc – have been carefully removed from his pockets. While the individual with a genuine dissociation disorder usually recovers his memory within a week or two with no more treatment than a safe, sympathetic environment for the time, the pretender's memory does not return until it is forced upon him.

Apart from stress avoidance the dissociative form of psychologically-mediated major memory loss can also occur in association with severe depression, epilepsy, multiple sclerosis, alcoholism or after head injury. However, there seems to be an important psychological element even when there are also organic factors. Recovery is usually as complete in these as it is in the purely psychological situations.

TRANSIENT GLOBAL AMNESIA

This neurological condition is dealt with more fully in the Neurology volume in this series. However, a psychiatrist is sometimes asked by a GP or Casualty Officer to see a case of this condition before diagnosis.

Transient global amnesia usually affects those in late-middle age or early old age, with a preponderance of males. There is a sudden halt to immediate and short-term memory functions, so that the patient cannot remember where he is or why, no matter how many times he is told. He remains alert and able to communicate rationally, apart from the memory deficit. He is likely to be puzzled or alarmed at what is happening to him. Memory gradually returns over a few hours, leaving no sequelae apart from a gap for the period of the attack.

The condition is thought to be vascular in origin, possibly related to migraine, but, because the patients invariably recover, there has been no opportunity for autopsy. There is no specific treatment and none is necessary since transient global amnesia is not psychogenic and most patients only ever have one attack and make a full recovery subsequently.

CHAPTER TEN

ALCOHOL, SOCIAL AND MEDICAL DRUGS

'I'm here in the Clink for a thundering drink and blacking the Corporal's eye.' So said Kipling's soldier, demonstrating the legal hazards of substance abuse. Alcohol is far and away the most important drug met with in psychiatry and in the courts. Either acute or chronic excessive intake can lead to trouble.

Legal problems associated with alcohol and some other substances

- driving offences;
- drunk and disorderly, drunk and incapable;
- assault;
- criminal damage;
- homicide, particularly in Scotland;
- petty crime;
- theft;
- vagrancy;
- domestic violence, battered wives;
- child abuse, child neglect;
- industrial accidents.

There may also be numerous psychiatric, social and medical problems.

ALCOHOL

Epidemiology for the United Kingdom

(This is similar in the United States.)

- 10% of the population has problems related to alcohol: this has been on the increase in the United Kingdom but not in the United States for the last 15 years;
- males are affected three times as often as females, and consume three times as much: in Asian and Hispanic cultures the ratio is 10:1;
- 30% of medical admissions to hospital are alcohol-related;
- 10% of psychiatric admissions are due to alcohol;
- 65% of accidents in the home involve alcohol;

- 41% of fatal road accidents involve alcohol;
- there is two and a half times as much absenteeism among problems drinkers as other workers;
- annual consumption of alcohol in the United Kingdom is half that in France, and indeed less than in all other European countries.

Risk factors for alcohol problems

Those most likely to become alcoholics are men in their late teens and early twenties, and in general those under 45. Unmarried, divorced or separated men or women are more susceptible, and the homeless have a particularly high rate of alcoholic problems: it is difficult to say which problem usually comes first.

Race, religion and cultural background have an influence: Western world Christians, apart from strict Baptists, have the highest incidence. The Irish are particularly vulnerable, while Jewish, Afro-Caribbean (and black Americans), Hindu, Moslem, Asian and Oriental people are less likely to encounter problems with alcohol. Family factors include a genetic predisposition to become dependent on alcohol: those affected usually start drinking heavily in teenage years. The family environment and, for boys especially, the role model of male drinking is important. A key factor is availability.

Occupations carrying a high risk

- bartender;
- brewery worker;
- seaman;
- journalist;
- printer;
- doctor;
- actor;
- businessmen with expense accounts.

Reasons for drinking

- social lubricant, pleasure;
- tranquillising effects in anxiety, social phobia, after trauma, with personal problems: men, in particular, often view alcohol as a panacea;
- physically, to alleviate pain, aid sleep;

- withdrawal symptoms, not only from alcohol but other drugs of dependency, such as heroin.

Pints, measures and units

One unit is equivalent to half a pint of beer, a glass of sherry, a glass of wine or a single pub measure of spirits (in Scotland a single provides 1.5 units).

1 bottle of spirits provides 30 units.

1 bottle of table wine provides 7 units.

1 bottle of sherry or port provides 15 units.

Recommended maximum

For men 21 units per week.

For women 14 units per week.

High risk

For men more than 50 units a week.

For women more than 35 units a week.

Driving

Legal limit 80 mg/100ml blood.

Risk of traffic accident: increased at 50 mg;

doubled at 80 mg;

increased tenfold at 100 mg/100ml.

PROBLEMS RELATED TO EXCESSIVE ALCOHOL CONSUMPTION

Acute intoxication

Psychiatric effects include easy emotionality with maudlin weeping, or the belligerence which leads to arrest for being 'drunk and disorderly'. Impulsive overdosing is common during a passing mood of self-pity. Judgment is impaired, leading to car and other accidents, and personal errors such as proposing marriage or lending large sums of money. This can be compounded by a 'memory black-out' for the previous evening despite carrying on a perfectly sensible conversation at the time. Several days together may be forgotten if the subject is taking part in a heavy bout of drinking.

Medical events include falls and fits, often involving head injury. There may be acute alcoholic poisoning with respiratory depression and inhalation of vomit, causing death.

Case: FD was a guardsman of 21 and extremely fit. He was accustomed to drinking eight or nine pints of beer most evenings, but, on this occasion, for a bet, he drank 21 single gins. He collapsed and was rushed to hospital by his friends, but died soon after admission. There was criticism of the bartender who had supplied so many drinks to one customer, but he excused himself by saying that he thought that several of the soldiers were drinking the gin.

Acute gastritis and oesophagitis, sometimes causing bleeding are commonplace, and other dangers are a reactive hypoglycaemia in a non-diabetic, and hypothermia although the subject feels warm and looks flushed. Acute myopathy and peripheral neuropathies affect others.

There are also a host of social and legal problems which occur with acute intoxication. Violence – 'fighting drunk' – may be domestic or in a public place, and can lead to criminal damage at best and homicide at worst. Being drunk is no defence. Sexual or other child abuse, usually by a man, or gross neglect of a child, usually by a woman, are other serious dangers. A man's sexual performance is often impaired, with problems in both erection and ejaculation, which increases his befuddled frustration. Marital dysharmony is inevitable. Turning up at work intoxicated or absenteeism for the same reason rapidly lead to dismissal.The Tory MP, Sir Nicholas Scott, lost the support of his constituents and the chance of standing in the next election by getting drunk at the Party Conference in 1996: he was found drunk and incapable in the street. Like others dependent on a substance, alcoholics sometimes steal to buy drink.

Chronic excess

This ranges from heavy drinking, the problem drinkers, to the alcohol-dependent, and accounts for most of the trouble. Unchecked, it is associated with a disastrous career.

Case

CW was typical. His drinking habit was well-established by his early twenties, and as a good sportsman he was popular. He seemed to be able to cope with the drinking without any adverse effects. His employers thought well of him and his career was set fair. His social drinking had escalated into regular heavy drinking by his late twenties, by which time he was living with his girlfriend and they were planning a family. It was in his early thirties that things began to go wrong, involving work, family and social difficulties. Declining efficiency and increasing unreliability led to the loss of his first, second and third jobs, each being of a lower grade than the one before. It was at the age of 37 that CW finally realised that he had lost control of his drinking and that his drinking was controlling him.

Most drinkers at this stage become deceptive, for instance secreting quarter bottles of vodka wherever they are. They have learned that it is difficult to detect the smell of vodka on someone's breath. Self-certificated sick leave mysteriously crops up on Mondays, after the weekend's drinking. Physical health begins to show a slow deterioration at this point. Health, job, family and home may all be lost and death is likely in the mid- to late-fifties.

Psychiatric effects of chronic alcohol excess

Mood disorders: these are the most obvious. A normally sociable, friendly person can become irritable and morose and waves of depression may push him into serious suicidal attempts. Between 6 and 20% of alcoholics die by suicide. As well as depression, heavy drinkers are prone to anxiety. Although people drink for 'Dutch courage' the end result is increased fearfulness. Even those with anti-social leanings, who drink before committing violent crimes, do not achieve mental calm and confidence. Apart from generalised anxiety, some drinkers develop specific, unreasonable phobias.

Suicidal risk is increased by unemployment, medical illness and lack of social and family support. Young men are at particular risk if they are either alcoholics or abuse other drugs or both.

Change of personality for the worse is the usual development, with increasing lack of concern for other people. The patient's most important relationship is with alcohol. Standards of conduct decline, with the neglect of responsibilities at home and at work. Uncharacteristic dishonesty and deceptiveness creep in.

Paranoid states start with taking offence over trivia and a generally suspicious outlook, leading to misinterpretations and finally the conviction that others are plotting to harm him. In his novel The Ordeal of Gilbert Pinfold, Evelyn Waugh describes such a case brilliantly.

Morbid or pathological jealousy may come over the drinker and he may suspect his sexual partner of infidelity. Occasionally this reaches delusional force, a highly dangerous condition. Of the homicidal patients admitted to Broadmoor Special Hospital in the 1960s 12% of the men and 15% of the women suffered from pathological jealousy. The prognosis for recovery is unpromising, with more than half the patients continuing to have groundless feelings of jealousy 10 years later. Since relapse tends to occur after discharge from hospital it is the psychiatrist's duty to warn the spouse of a substantial risk of violence.

Case

NM, an engineer, had originally come from Nigeria, where he had suffered persecution on political grounds. He was in his mid-thirties and had been married for three years to an Englishwoman, but they had no children. He acquired a social drinking habit which rapidly ran into heavy drinking, although he was seldom drunk. He began to have symptoms of gastritis. These did not respond to simple measures, largely because his drinking continued as before.

Suddenly, with no precipitant, NM had a blinding insight: he 'knew for certain' that his wife was trying to poison him by putting faeces in his food. He could taste it. He was convinced that she had another man and wanted to dispose of him. When his doctor had tried to reason with him, having discussed the matter with the wife, NM immediately believed that the GP was in the plot and refused to see him. He complained at the local police station, but as he smelled of alcohol, he was merely reassured. Since NM believed that there was no other way of preserving his own life and punishing his wife, he decided that he must kill her.

Apart from the delusional system concerning his wife, NM's reasoning and behaviour were normal, and he planned the murder – by electrocution in the bath – carefully.

By a thousand to one chance, there was a local power cut at the critical time, and NM came back from the pub that evening to find his wife still alive but puzzled by some wires attached to the bath. His surprise at seeing her as usual, and recalling his recent nagging about what men she had seen in the day made her realise that her husband's thinking was seriously disturbed, and she escaped to a friend's house. NM was admitted to hospital compulsorily, under Section 2 of the Mental Health Act and this was later converted to Section 3 to allow for longer detention and treatment (see Chapter 12). Had the matter reached court, for instance if Mrs NM had been killed or injured and NM had been charged with attempted murder, the judge or the defence counsel would have asked for a psychiatric assessment. Although NM presented as normal and rational most of the time, he would have been likely to show his paranoia when he was questioned about his wife. Although he did not have a schizophrenic illness, it was clear that he was psychotic, had lost touch with reality and that treatment in hospital would be more appropriate than imprisonment. Mrs NM would never be safe when her husband was at large.

There is often a regrettable and dangerousness laxness about informing the person likely to be at risk when a potentially dangerous patient or prisoner is released.

Alcoholic hallucinosis: in this condition the patient, in clear consciousness, hears hallucinatory voices uttering threats or insults. The outlook is poor, and the condition often progresses into schizophrenia, or the amnesic syndrome and then dementia.

Alcoholic dementia: this is associated with long-term alcohol abuse causing brain atrophy. The neurones are not killed, but lose their connecting dendrites and cannot function. However, abstinence for upwards of three years occasionally produces some improvement, unlike the inexorable progression of other dementias.

Withdrawal symptoms: these develop and worsen rapidly 8–12 hours after the last drink and rage for three or four days, or occasionally a week. Surgeons especially may be caught unawares and mistake the withdrawal phenomena for infection or some other untoward result of the operation.

The symptoms are:

- anxiety, restlessness, terror – 'the horrors';
- tremor, staggering gait;
- fever, nausea, sweating – these symptoms can lead to misdiagnosis initially;
- visual hallucinations, typically on day one;
- disorientation in time, place and person;
- paranoid delusions.

There is a risk of death if the condition is not adequately treated, from intercurrent infection, circulatory collapse or suicide. For the unwary doctor there is the danger of inadvertent negligence if the situation is not realised promptly.

Wernicke's encephalopathy: this presents suddenly with mental confusion, staggering, and ocular difficulties with nystagmus. It is basically due to thiamine deficiency. This in turn is caused by a diet deficient in whole wheat, meat, fresh fruit and vegetables, such as that of many alcoholics: the body has hardly any storage capacity for thiamine, so a constant supply is needed. In addition, in drinkers, absorption from the gut is impaired, storage is impaired, and the metabolism of large quantities of alcohol uses up excessive amounts of the vitamin.

The encephalopathy often responds to prompt, vigorous treatment with thiamine, but failure to diagnose the syndrome is disastrous.

Korsakoff's psychosis: this is the residual effect of inadequately treated or untreated Wernicke's encephalopathy, and is usually permanent. The main characteristic feature is the inability to learn anything new (see p 83). High dose thiamine administration is occasionally helpful if started early.

SOCIAL DRUGS

People take illegal or prescribed drugs in excess for various reasons:

- to calm their anxieties and help them to sleep: usually older people;
- to stimulate them so that they can party all night without fatigue;
- to induce interesting mental experiences and changes of perception;
- to produce a feeling of euphoria – well-being and happiness.

Drugs in common use

Cannabis: this is very widely used, for example 13% of the population of the United States are estimated to use cannabis. It is supplied as the dried vegetable, marijuana or grass, or the resin. It tends to enhance the current mood and usually produces a state of dreamy relaxation in which all effort is postponed – the mañana effect. There is also a subtle change in perception which can be disturbing for drivers. In some sensitive young people it can induce anxiety, paranoia or confusion, and in a few this appears to lead to the permanent disability of schizophrenia. It does not cause physical dependency, but there may be a psychological craving.

Heroin: this is the most important drug of abuse, particularly since the advent of AIDS. There are 20,000 registered heroin users in the UK, with as many again who are not registered. Medically, heroin is used for its excellent analgesic effects. Illegally it is used for its equally powerful euphoriant effect, especially when injected directly into a vein. This route is fraught with the risk of introducing the HIV virus, and has had devastating results in Edinburgh.

Tolerance develops rapidly, so the dosage escalates. There is a trap if the drug is stopped for any length of time, for instance in prison. Tolerance evaporates as quickly as it builds up and many deaths have been caused by the user's returning to the dose that had previously been 'safe'. Death is due to respiratory depression. Withdrawal symptoms include unbearable craving, cramps, vomiting and diarrhoea, running eyes and nose and disrupted temperature control. The symptoms start 4–6 hours after the last dose and continue for up to 48 hours.

Because of the intensity of the withdrawal effects, heroin users build their lives round getting their next 'fix', and much street crime is prompted by the urgent need for money. Methadone is often used to replace heroin as maintenance treatment, since there is 36 hours 'grace' before withdrawal symptoms become severe.

Amphetamines, eg speed: these are used as stimulants either alone or with a narcotic, and improperly as slimming pills. They are legally available on prescription for attention deficit disorder in children and the rare disorder, narcolepsy. The effects desired by social users are general stimulation of the central nervous system, with mild euphoria and absence of fatigue, so that you can stay awake all weekend, and not even feel hungry. The 'let-down' effect after taking amphetamines includes depression, occasionally to the point of suicide, anxiety and craving for more. Tolerance develops rapidly.

With chronic use a paranoid psychosis, closely resembling schizophrenia, may come on out of the blue, with particular emphasis on visual hallucinations. The psychosis usually, but not invariably, subsides over 10 days. There is also the physical effect of raised blood pressure: a serious matter for some middle-aged, overweight people, using amphetamines for slimming. Similar reactions have been described with other such stimulants as phenmetrazine, methylphenidate and pemoline. Any doctor tempted to dally with prescribing pills for slimming risks not only claims for negligence, but criminal charges.

Cocaine: this has effects similar to those of amphetamines: increased energy, excitement, euphoria with grandiose ideas. Large doses can lead to sexual disinhibition and paranoid ideas which make the person aggressive. This state of mind may develop into a short-lived paranoid psychosis, marked by violence. Physical effects centre on increased pulse rate and raised blood pressure.

Cocaine is intensely addictive. It can be injected, smoked or sniffed. Crack cocaine is purified cocaine derived from the street product; it has an extremely rapid effect, especially if inhaled. Its use has increased dramatically in the UK over the last decade, particularly in the 18–25 year old age group. Tolerance readily develops. The 'crash' that supervenes when cocaine is withdrawn involves feelings of total misery and the pointlessness of life, anxiety, irritability, exhaustion and hypersomnia: excessive sleep.

MDMA: ecstasy: this synthetic preparation, 3,4 methylenedioxymet-amphetamine, is a mix of stimulant and hallucinogen. One 120 mg tablet or capsule is effective for 4–6 hours and produces a happy, friendly state with a feeling of intimacy, heightened perception and a sense of having just discovered wonderful insights into the meaning of life.

Tolerance soon develops, and with increased dosage various ill-effects are increasingly likely, although some individuals can get these effects idiosyncratically with a single dose. Hyperthermia (severely raised temperature), disturbances of the cardiac rhythm, and bleeding within the brain may occur, with fatal outcome. Both acute and chronic paranoid psychoses are described with continued use of the drug, as are 'flashbacks': spontaneous re-occurrences of the feeling of having taken a dose.

Hallucinogens: these occur naturally, for instance in 'magic mushrooms' and also, mildly, with cannabis. Synthetics include ecstasy (above), dimethyltriptamine, and LSD.

Lysergic acid diethylamide (LSD): The effects come on over two hours and last for 8–14 hours. Perceptions in every modality may be distorted and seem to have deep significance. Time appears to move very slowly. Distortions of the body image in particular may cause distress, panic and a fear of going mad. The mood varies from dread to exhilaration.

Case

PL, a music student at Cambridge, experimented with LSD while seeking inspiration. The first couple of times she felt that she was on the verge of doing something wonderful, but on the third occasion she was filled with terror and jumped from a second floor window to escape. The main damage was to her pelvis, apart from losing her place at the University. She spent eight weeks in hospital, suffering occasional flashbacks, and was then discharged to outpatient follow-up. She had been out for two days when she had a severe flashback and took a non-fatal overdose. She then sued the orthopaedic surgeon and the psychiatrist who had looked after her in hospital for medical negligence. They had failed to ensure that she would be supervised when she left hospital, knowing that she might be subject to flashbacks. The defence suggested that she might have taken another dose of LSD when she was out, and that her attack was a real, self-induced trip, not a flashback. This defence was not accepted but the doctor and surgeon were criticised for failing to communicate with PL's GP before she was discharged.

The peak age for taking LSD is 26–34, which is relatively mature, and most regular users take precautions against the dangers of a 'bad trip' by ensuring that someone else is present throughout. Tolerance and dependence are rare.

Solvents: glue-sniffing first became a problem in Britain in the 1970s, although solvents had long been part of the drug scene in the United States. Solvents are usually used by a group of youngsters together, mainly boys of 8–19, with a peak from 13–15. In a recent survey in the United States, it was found that 7% of schoolchildren had inhaled solvents at some time during the last year. The substances used are numerous and easily available. They include glue, petrol, cleaning fluids, various aerosols, butane, toluene and the agents in fire extinguishers.

Solvents can induce a feeling of happy relaxation, sometimes with hallucinations, rather like being drunk. Among the less desirable effects are slurring of speech, unsteady gait, nausea and vomiting. There is also a significant risk of sudden death: 100 children annually die in the UK from solvent abuse. The causes are heart failure and respiratory depression.

LEGAL ASPECTS OF SUBSTANCE ABUSE

Users may commit crimes for ready cash to fund their habit, but also when they are under the influence of alcohol or another drug and are not in full control. Legally, a person is fully responsible for his actions after knowingly taking these substances. The Mental Health Act 1983 specifically excludes simple alcohol or (often illegal) substance abuse from classification as mental illness, although such substances may cause disinhibition and loss of memory. The effects of drugs taken voluntarily are no defence in law for criminal offences.

The exception is 'involuntary intoxication' which can arise in several ways:

1   *Deception*: the person has been tricked into taking a substance without his knowledge: easy to claim, but very difficult to prove.

2   *Idiosyncratic reaction*: an unusual, individual response to a substance, which could not have been anticipated. Manie a Poitu is an example: a small dose of alcohol leads to disorientation and a brief outburst of violence, followed by sleep and no memory of the event. It is more likely if there has been a previous head injury. Lawyers and psychiatrists are divided as to the validity of the concept, but it has been offered as a defence. In most cases it will fail.

3   *Untoward and unexpected reaction to a legally prescribed drug*: for example, a taxi driver charged with careless driving and causing an accident claimed that he was in a daze from the effects of taking 30 mg of flurazepam, a long-acting hypnotic the night before. His doctor, knowing the man's occupation, should have been meticulous in ensuring that the driver knew that he should not drive if he still felt any effects from the drug on the following day. It was in the afternoon that the accident occurred, but it was judged that the taxi driver, with his responsible job, should have realised that he was not fully alert.

Case

Miss CK, 47, suffered from pulmonary sarcoid, a chronic disorder which left her with a much reduced respiratory reserve. A small dose of the glucocorticoid, prednisolone, usually helped her through the winter months. In January she was just starting a new secretarial post on a three-months' trial period. She was particularly anxious, in view of her age, to appear to be capable of doing the job. Unfortunately she developed a simple respiratory infection which made her distressingly and obviously short of breath. She went to her doctor.

An increase in her steroid dosage helped her breathing, but two days later she accused her new boss of plotting to rape and murder her, and attacked him with a paper knife. The police and a psychiatrist were both called. There had been no mental disorder in Miss CK's personal or family history, and the steroid medication was blamed for her behaviour. In this case her employer withdrew the charges, and Miss CK rapidly recovered with psychiatric treatment and necessarily gradual reduction of the steroid. The severity of the symptoms in such cases are not directly dependent on the dosage, but should subside soon after the medication has been withdrawn.

For this type of involuntary intoxication to be accepted as a defence there has to be a clear chronological link between the medication and the offence, and the patient's behaviour cannot have been due to any illness, for instance schizophrenia, from which the patient was already suffering.

4   *Incapable of intent*: for this defence the offender must show that he was so severely intoxicated by the substance he has taken that he could not possibly have formed the intent to do the criminal act.

The rule is that the court will not accept this plea for crimes of basic intent: such as manslaughter, assault and unlawful wounding. The accused person will not be acquitted however intoxicated he was, if he knowingly and willingly took the substance in question. Crimes of specific intent such as murder or theft may be assessed more leniently if the offender can be shown to have been unable to form a definite intention to commit that crime because of the action of some substance. A charge of murder may be reduced to manslaughter, carrying a lesser sentence.

Case

L had taken LSD when he was in bed with his girlfriend. He 'woke' from the effects of the drug as from a nightmare, and found that he had throttled her. He had been in a hallucinatory state in which he believed he was fending off the attack of numerous snakes. He was charged with murder, but the case went to the Court of Appeal and he was found guilty of the lesser offence of manslaughter (Lipman (1969) 53 Cr App R 60).

Prescribed medication that may cause psychiatric symptoms and lead to violent or other offences

Psychotic symptoms with delusions and/or hallucinations, mimicking schizophrenia: appetite suppressants, steroids including those used irregularly by athletes, levodopa, beta-blockers, indomethacin, anticholinergics such as benzhexol, sympathomimetics such as pseudoepinephrine (as in cold cures).

Disorientation, delirium: central nervous system depressants including sleeping tablets, sedatives, anti-depressants, major tranquillisers, antihistamines, anti-convulsants, and alcohol; anti-cholinergics, beta-blockers, cimetidine, digoxin.

Depression: steroids, anti-hypertensives, anti-convulsants, major tranquillisers, oral contraceptives, levodopa.

Manic elation: steroids, anti-depressants, anti-cholinergics, isoniazid.

Strange or violent behaviour: benzodiazepines such as diazepam, major tranquillisers as such chlorpromazine.

These drugs do not cause untoward effects in the great majority of patients in therapeutic doses: there has to be a special sensitivity. For example, the elderly may react in an unexpected way to something as simple as an over-the-counter cold medicine, and, for example, shop-lift in a confused state.

CHAPTER ELEVEN

PARANOID SYNDROMES

The term 'paranoid' comes from two Greek words: *para* (beside) and *nous* (mind). To an ancient Greek paranoid meant 'out of his mind' or mad. Nowadays the word has persecutory connotations which were introduced by a group of German and Austrian psychiatrists 100 years ago. One of them was Eugen Bleuler who introduced the concept of paranoid schizophrenia. Freud put paranoia down to repressed sex, in this case homosex.

Paranoid ideas and beliefs are of particular interest to medico-legal practitioners, since they can impel those who hold them into assault on another person, often someone perfectly blameless. Since the Care in the Community programme has replaced the old asylum concept, there have been a number of cases of violence involving psychiatric patients with paranoid disorders.

Types of paranoid thinking

Paranoid delusions: these are the most important because they are the most dangerous. They are loosely termed 'false beliefs'. The patient holds an absolute and incontrovertible conviction of the truth of his delusion but to others, even other patients with delusions of their own, it seems implausible and irrational. A psychotically deluded patient may believe that the CIA are spying on his every move, that an infernal machine has been concealed in his house, or that rays from Mars are directed at him. If the police and the GP do not appear to take his complaints seriously, this is likely to be seen as evidence of their complicity in some evil plot to harm him.

Overvalued ideas: these are deeply held personal convictions which preoccupy the person's mind, but may be understandable when the patient's background is examined. They may be unusual or exaggerated but they are not bizarre.

Ideas of reference: unduly sensitive, self-conscious individuals may feel sure that everyone has been talking about them in a derogatory way when they come into a room, and have remarked on something shameful about them, for instance that they smell. The person has a fleeting idea that his fears may be out of proportion, but cannot put them out of his mind. This condition has similarities to an obsessional neurosis.

Delusions of reference: these differ from ideas of reference in their delusional intensity and unshakeability. The victim 'sees' references to himself and his personal life in the newspapers, on the television, or even in the colour change of traffic lights.

Grandiose delusions: the patient believes that he is someone of great importance, frequently royal.

Case

Mr GO, a Nigerian, was convinced that he was the rightful heir to the British throne and frequently made a scene outside Buckingham Palace, demanding entry and immediate coronation as King George VII. He showed no other symptoms of psychiatric abnormality so he could not legally be compelled to go into a psychiatric hospital, or even to take medication. Nevertheless, the magistrates felt unable to give Mr GO a custodial sentence, so his behaviour continued until he moved to Manchester.

WHO HAS PARANOID IDEAS OR BELIEFS?

Paranoid personalities: such people, constitutionally or because of their early life experience, have always been introverted, sensitive and suspicious. It may not be until middle life, perhaps after some stress, that these traits lead to problems and some particular persecutory idea becomes fixed. Childhood illness, lack of siblings and later isolation all aggravate the tendency.

Case

Miss ST, an unmarried woman in her fifties, with a post of some responsibility in the Home Office, made constant complaints to the local council and the police about her next-door neighbours. She insisted that were pursuing a policy of deliberate harassment by hoovering or undertaking carpentry every night, when they judged that she had just got to sleep. When she had been woken up they would stop the noise, only to start again when she next began to sleep. Naturally, neither the noise abatement officer nor the police ever heard it. Things improved temporarily when the neighbours moved, but while their flat was empty Miss ST reported hearing squatters moving about in it at night.

Difficulties between neighbours are a fruitful source of litigation, and in some cases call for a psychiatric assessment.

Paranoid states or disorders: these merge imperceptibly with paranoid personalities, although the underlying personality problem may only be recognised with hindsight. A paranoid *state* (ICD-10) or paranoid *disorder* (DSM-IV) is classified as a psychiatric illness, on the borders of psychosis. The ideas of persecution may reach delusional force but they are not part of a schizophrenic or manic-depressive psychosis. The other manifestations of these disorders are notably absent and the patient is well able to function normally.

The one-track paranoid idea frequently concerns a female neighbour, or is to do with sexual jealousy in a man, in some cases, but not all, associated with alcohol (see p 97). Paranoia can impinge even more directly on medicine. It is not unusual for a patient to have a preoccupying concern about some part of his body which he perceives as abnormal. This may underlie the patient's badgering for plastic surgery. It is more worrying when a delusion develops following some medical procedure.

Case

Mrs AS, 37, had surgery for the removal of a benign but bulky ovarian cyst. Her operation coincided with a lot of publicity about a young child who had been discharged from hospital after a minor operation with a metal clip still inside him. Mrs AS had some post-operative discomfort which was slow to settle and she became convinced that she could feel something hard underneath the scar. When an X-ray was negative, she said perhaps it was something plastic. Mrs AS was so plausible and determined that the senior registrar who had performed the operation began to have doubts. Mrs AS approached a solicitor to start proceedings. However, neither of the consultant gynaecologists called in for the prosecution and the defence could find any physical cause for Mrs AS' ongoing discomfort.

Her solicitor advised her to consult a psychiatrist. She was furious at the suggestion, but her husband managed to persuade her. A trial period on a major tranquillizer improved her discomfort and also helped to lessen the strength of her delusion.

PARANOID PSYCHOSES

In contrast to paranoid personalities and paranoid states, paranoid psychoses are definite illnesses with a clear-cut onset and, if successfully treated, ending. In these disorders the patient often experiences hallucinations of voices abusing or threatening him, making a derisory running commentary on his most private activities, or plotting his destruction. In some of the cases associated with a physical illness there may also be clouding of consciousness.

There are two broad categories of paranoid psychoses: those with organic causes and those which are part and parcel of a schizophrenic, manic-depressive or schizo-affective disorder.

Organic types

Intoxications

Amphetamine psychosis closely mimics acute schizophrenia (see p 113 below and also Chapter 10). Abusive hallucinatory voices are especially common and the patient is very restless.

LSD occasionally produces a paranoid psychosis, usually without 'the voices' but with feelings of being controlled by an outside force.

Alcoholic hallucinosis usually combines critical voices with intense anxiety.

None of these paranoid reactions lasts more than a few months, while in most cases the duration is two or three weeks. Anything lasting much longer raises the question of whether the drug or drink has precipitated a schizophrenic illness. Patients suffering any of these disorders are liable to unpredictable outbursts of violence. Hallucinatory voices of an insulting or threatening nature are often the trigger to assault. In most of these substance-abuse cases, in the absence of an incipient or underlying serious psychiatric disorder such as schizophrenia, a plea of diminished responsibility or a recommendation for psychiatric treatment rather than punishment may not succeed.

Case

DY, a 50 year old clerk in a City bank, was a heavy and continuous drinker, although he had never publically disgraced himself by getting drunk. However, he did develop alcoholic hallucinosis. He was going through the barrier at Liverpool Street station when he heard a man's voice accusing him of various obscene sexual practices. He turned round and hit the man just behind him, breaking his nose and his glasses. Witnesses came forward who had seen the apparently unprovoked assault and DY was charged but was still complaining of the words he had heard when he got to court. The magistrate asked for a psychiatric report.

On questioning by the psychiatrist DY admitted that he had heard these rude voices several times during the last month or two, usually when he was in a public place such as the station, where there was a good deal of background noise. He had also experienced some problems with his memory. There was no history of schizophrenia in DY's family nor in his personal background. Since this was a relatively chronic psychotic condition rather than an acute effect of alcohol, DY was put on probation on the understanding that he would co-operate with psychiatric treatment.

Chronic organic reactions

Acute organic reactions such as delirium tremens are often characterised by terrifying visual or auditory hallucinations, known as 'the horrors', which may make the patient violent in supposed self-defence, but these disorders are short-lived and the patient is so obviously ill that there is no necessity to involve the law. Some cases develop into chronic conditions which may be more difficult to diagnose.

Dementias: in the early stages of these degenerative disorders, when the situation is not clear, the patients are frequently subject to paranoid suspicions and may hit out. This is particularly likely in Huntington's chorea, since the patient is likely to be relatively young – in his thirties or forties – and may be adept at hiding other symptoms of the disease. Aggression is typical of the post-traumatic dementia which may follow serious head injury.

Brain tumour or other space-occupying lesion within the skull: those in the temporal region are notoriously associated with emotional instability and aggressive behaviour, while in the frontal area there is gross disinhibition so that there may be reckless and inappropriate behaviour.

Endocrine disorders: the thyroid diseases, myxoedema and hyperthyroidism, can provoke a paranoid-depressive psychosis. A similar picture may arise in Cushing's syndrome: hallucinations are common in a setting of excitement.

Case

A GP's wife is described by Dr AD Forest. At 26 she became continually angry, unlike her previous calm self, and was abusive to the patients and to her husband. She suspected him of nefarious activities whenever he was called out in the evening or at weekends, and was threatening divorce. She slept badly and was tense and restless in the day. She had also lost several kilogrammes in weight despite a good appetite. It was this latter circumstance which was the clue which led to a blood test and a diagnosis of thyrotoxicosis. This was effectively treated over the next few months and her weight and personality were restored.

Paranoid psychosis in the elderly: vague suspiciousness and ideas of self-reference are not unusual in the elderly, especially those living alone, slightly deaf and with incipient cognitive decline. Misinterpretations happen easily, and if something is mislaid, the senior citizen may feel sure that someone has taken it. It is small step from this to developing an idea that someone, often a neighbour or relative, is persecuting him.

Case

Mrs GL, 72, a long-time widow, kept noticing a yellow van outside her block of flats. She concluded that the villain who had hidden her purse, and put the butter out when she was sure that she had put it in the fridge, was waiting and watching her flat from the van (it belonged, in fact, to the electricity company). She always found that her things had been moved a few inches when she came back from a shopping trip, or that a light had been turned on when she was sure she had switched it off. She is at risk of being accused of wasting police time by reporting burglaries which have no basis in fact. It is only if she gets into a dispute that her paranoid state will be recognised. Neuroleptic treatment would, at least, enable her to feel less anxious.

Erotomania: stalker's disorder: also called de Clerambault's syndrome. This condition has achieved a good deal of publicity recently, and has been the reason for the establishment in law of a new criminal offence. De Clerambault, a French physician, published his book, *Les psychoses passionelles*, in 1942, and one well-known case that he described was of a woman who haunted Buckingham Palace because of a passion for King George V, which she believed was returned. Other cases, from the Greek, Perdiccas, onwards have been described through the ages. These early cases were a rarity and the stalker was considered to be psychotic, or mad. The majority of stalkers were women.

In the last 10 years, however, stalking has become much more common and the majority who come to attention are men. These stalkers are more likely to be dangerous and although some cases are recognised as definitely psychotic, suffering from a variant of paranoid schizophrenia, most stalkers are regarded by the laity as common offenders, deserving of punishment. This may sometimes be unfair and it is worth the time for a defence lawyer to explore the possibility of serious mental illness. This could be used in mitigation or to get more appropriate treatment for the person concerned.

The stalker is typically lonely and sexually frustrated, often above average intelligence and commonly unemployed. This enables him to follow his victim, research his background and write and and telephone her constantly. The calls and letters are liable to become increasingly threatening and the victim's life is made unbearable. As long ago as 1983, before stalking became newsworthy, of 112 men convicted of violent offences, four were found to be stalkers. The victim is frequently, but not necessarily, someone well-known with whom he is barely acquainted, if at all. What begins as an erotic obsession with an unrealistic hope of fulfilment switches to resentment and unyielding hatred when the victim does not respond. A characteristic of stalkers is their pride.

Case

David Greenhalgh, a 33 year old married solicitor, was stalked for two years by a client, a 41 year old nurse, also married, who wanted to marry him. In 1996 she was arrested and charged with assault, after throwing petrol over Mr Greenhalgh's receptionists, whom she blamed for keeping them apart. She was detained in a psychiatric hospital.

Treatment with anti-psychotic medication affords some control of the disorder but only for as long as the subject takes the medication. In general, erotomanic delusions are as immovable as any others by persuasion or punishment. Custodial sentences at least give the victim some respite, but are often irrelevant in producing a change in the patient's thinking.

Paranoid schizophrenia: this is the paranoid illness par excellence. It is the commonest type of schizophrenia, which is itself the most important and widespread mental illness, affecting all races, and the most likely to be associated with crimes of violence. It is classified F20.0 in ICD-10 and 295.30 in DSM-IV.

Schizophrenia has a point-prevalence of 2-5-5.3 per 1,000 of the European population and affects the sexes equally. The usual age of onset is between 15 and 45, with males affected several years earlier than females.

Symptoms include:

- voices speaking to the patient, making a running commentary about him or two or more persons discussing him;
- suspiciousness and secretiveness;
- a sense of danger, and something important about to happen;
- a feeling that his thoughts are being siphoned off;
- his thoughts may seem to be spoken aloud (not by him), or otherwise made available to everyone;
- delusions of persecution, often by a group or organisation, for instance the Freemasons, the government, or a tenants' association;
- disordered thoughts: odd, jarring lapses of logic crop up in conversation, for instance that the car is going faster because it has just been filled with petrol.

The patient has no insight and, as the Nazis discovered, even torture is unable to make him abandon his delusional beliefs.

The previous personality may have been normal, but in the prodromal phase there is often withdrawal from social activities and deterioration in the patient's work, study and general functioning.

Schizophrenia is such a serious illness, with such devastating effects on thought and belief, that an offender charged with a violent, apparently motiveless crime against person or property is likely to be remanded for a psychiatric report, and to be sent to a psychiatric hospital, a medium secure unit or a Special Hospital such as Broadmoor or Rampton if he is found to have paranoid schizophrenic illness. An exception was Sutcliffe, the Yorkshire Ripper. Although the psychiatrists for the defence and the prosecution agreed on the diagnosis of paranoid schizophrenia, public opinion was so strong that he was sentenced to imprisonment, at least initially.

Schizophrenia can affect anyone and does not impair their intelligence, so there have been cases of practising solicitors and hospital doctors apparently working normally and managing to conceal violent or other abnormal behaviour associated with their delusions, for years. The artist Richard Dadd, while painting the most beautiful and serene pictures, killed his father believing him to be the devil incarnate, and later, for a similar reason, attempted to murder a man who happened to share the same train compartment with him. He spent the rest of his life in the Bethlem Hospital, still painting.

Treatment: in most cases medication provides some control of the disease, and many of the recent cases of violence on discharge from hospital have been due to the patient discontinuing treatment.

Manic-depressive psychosis: this is the other major mental illness involving delusions and, occasionally, hallucinations. The essence of the disorder is in severe mood changes, either to depression with a high risk of suicide or to mania or hypomania when the patient may believe that he is someone of great importance, even Jesus Christ or the Virgin Mary: voices may affirm his status and powers. Often, in a manic episode, the patient is irritable and may have paranoid ideas because other people do not treat him as his self-imposed importance demands.

Schizoaffective psychosis: this is a combination of the symptoms of schizophrenia and manic-depressive psychosis, and paranoid ideas and delusions are more likely than in the latter alone.

Paranoid disorders, particularly the psychoses, pose the greatest dangers from psychiatric patients, and it is important to investigate immediately any indication of such disorder where violence is threatened or attempted.

CHAPTER TWELVE

MENTAL HEALTH LAW

Those dealing with mentally abnormal patients have special responsibilities, to the patient and to the public. Because psychiatrists have powers not accorded to other practitioners, ie those of detaining a patient in hospital and giving him treatment against his will thus destroying his autonomy, the legal constraints are of vital importance. Psychiatric patients themselves are also unique in that their illness can make them dangerous to themselves and to the public, often in an unpredictable fashion.

The Mental Health Act 1983 is the cornerstone of the legislation regulating the care of the mentally disordered in England and Wales. It consolidates the Mental Health Act 1959 and the Mental Health (Amendment) Act 1982 and governs 'the reception, care and treatment of mentally disordered patients, the management of their property and other related matters'. The most important, and contentious part of the Act concerned the rules for compulsory detention and consent to treatment. The Mental Health Act Commission, an independent, multidisciplinary body, has the duty of overseeing and safeguarding the interests of patients who are compulsorily detained. It visits the patients, receives reports about their treatment, investigates complaints and appoints doctors and others concerned in mental health to advise on matters pertaining to consent to treatment.

Definitions for the Mental Health Act

Mental disorder means 'mental illness, arrested or incomplete development of mind, psychopathic disorder and any other disorder or disability of mind'.

Severe mental impairment means 'a state of arrested or incomplete development of mind which includes severe impairment of intelligence and social functioning and is associated with abnormally aggressive or severely irresponsible conduct'.

Mental impairment means 'a state of arrested or incomplete development of mind (not amounting to severe mental impairment) which includes significant impairment of intelligence and social functioning and is associated with abnormally aggressive or seriously irresponsible conduct'.

Psychopathic disorder means 'a persistent disorder or disability of mind (whether or not including significant impairment of intelligence) which results in abnormally aggressive or seriously irresponsible conduct on the part of the person concerned'.

Promiscuity or other immoral conduct, sexual deviancy or dependence on alcohol or drugs alone are specifically excluded from the definition of mental disorder.

For most purposes the term 'mental disorder' is insufficient as a diagnosis, and the patient must be assigned to one of the four categories above. However, for most (97%) of formal or compulsory admissions in the NHS the diagnosis given is 'mental illness' which is not defined in the Act, and it designated an operational term and its usage a matter of clinical judgment. Attempts have been made to pinpoint the essential features, and this near miss is a guide.

Mental illness is an illness showing one or more of the following characteristics:

- more than temporary impairment of intellectual functions, shown by a failure of memory, orientation, comprehension and learning capacity;
- more than temporary alteration of mood of such degree as to give rise to the patient having a delusional appraisal of his situation, his past or his future or that of others, or to the lack of any appraisal;
- delusional beliefs, persecutory, jealous or grandiose;
- abnormal perceptions associated with delusional misinterpretation of events;
- thinking so disordered as to prevent the patient making a reasonable appraisal of his situation or having reasonable communication with others.

Sections of the Act dealing with compulsory detention in hospital

Section 2: Application for admission for assessment (operative 28 days)

This is the most frequently used section when informal admission to hospital is not possible or is inappropriate. It can also include treatment, after the assessment has been made. The necessary conditions are:

1 The patient is suffering from a mental disorder which warrants his detention for assessment, or assessment followed by treatment.
2 Admission is necessary in the interest of the patient's own health or safety or for the protection of others.

Procedure

1 Application by the patient's nearest relative or an approved social worker who must have seen the patient within the last 14 days. The social worker should consult the nearest relative if possible, but often, to avoid later

recriminations by the patient, it is better if a social worker rather than a relative makes the application.

2   Medical recommendation by two doctors, one of whom is approved under Section 12 of the Act as having special experience and expertise in psychiatry. The two doctors should not be on the staff of the same hospital, unless it is likely to be unacceptably time-consuming to bring in an outside doctor. Ideally, and very often, the non-specialist doctor is the patient's GP. The two doctors must examine the patient with five days of each other.

Sections of the Act dealing with compulsory admission to hospital

Section 2 Admission for assessment or for assessment followed by medical treatment (runs for 28 days)

This section is the one most frequently used when informal, that is, voluntary, admission to a psychiatric ward or hospital is not possible or appropriate. The necessary conditions are:

1   The patient is suffering from a mental disorder that warrants his detention for assessment or assessment followed by treatment. (Even when the basic diagnosis, for instance schizophrenia, is well-known, assessment may be required regarding the current severity of the illness and any potentially dangerous symptoms.)

2   Admission is necessary in the interests of the patient's own health or safety or for the protection of others.

Procedure

1   Application is made by the patient's nearest relative or an approved social worker, who must have seen the patient within the last 14 days. The social worker should consult with the relative if possible. Often, to avoid later recriminations in the family, it is better if the social worker actually makes the application. The application goes to the managers of the hospital to which the patient is being admitted.

2   Medical recommendations are required by two doctors, one of whom is approved under Section 12 of the Act as having special knowledge and experience in mental disorder. The two doctors should not be on the staff of the same hospital unless it is likely to be unacceptably time-consuming to find an outside doctor. Ideally, and very often in practice, the non-specialist doctor is the patient's GP. The doctors must examine the patient within five days of each other.

Case

AL was a 27 year old teacher, unmarried but with a live-in partner. He went to see their doctor because he was worried by AL's severe and incomprehensible depression. It had come on over three or four days, and she was convinced against all argument that she was so evil that she was contaminating everyone else with disease, that she was responsible for CJD, the E.coli outbreaks and cholera in Bangladesh, and that she deserved to die. The GP, who knew something of the background, was alarmed and called in a local psychiatrist. There was a streak of manic-depressive illness in AL's family, and there had been several suicides, although AL herself had not been psychiatrically ill before. Neither of the doctors nor AL's partner were able to persuade her to go into hospital voluntarily: she believed that she would be executed there. The duty social worker was called upon, and the necessary forms completed. AL was not violent, so there was no need to have police assistance in transferring her to the hospital.

If the psychiatrist had not been readily available, and if AL had been actively threatening suicide, an emergency order might have been necessary instead of Section 2.

Section 4 Admission for assessment in cases of emergency (last for 72 hours)

An emergency application may be made either by an approved social worker who must have seen the patient within 24 hours, or the nearest relative, stating that it is urgently necessary for the patient to be admitted and that there would be undesirable delay in complying with the procedure for a Section 2 admission. A recommendation by one doctor is sufficient and he need not be on the approved list, but, if practicable, he should have had previous acquaintance with the patient. The patient must be admitted within 24 hours of being examined or of the application being made.

A second medical recommendation is required within the 72 hours to convert the Section 4 to a Section 2.

While most of these cases start off in the patient's home, with his GP, occasionally a Section 4 is applied in the Accident and Emergency Department of a hospital if a patient seems to be in imminent danger of harming himself or others.

Section 3 Admission for treatment (applies for six months in the first instance, renewable for a second six months, and yearly after that)

Grounds for an application for admission for treatment:

1   the patient is suffering from mental illness, severe mental impairment, psychopathic disorder or mental impairment and his disorder is of a nature or degree which makes it appropriate for him to receive treatment in hospital; and

2   in the case of psychopathic disorder or mental impairment, such treatment is likely to alleviate or prevent a deterioration of his condition; and it is

necessary for the health or safety of the patient or for the protection of other persons that he should receive such treatment and it cannot be provided unless he is detained under this section.

The application for admission is founded on the written recommendations of two doctors, on a prescribed form.

The patient may be discharged by order of the responsible medical officer, the hospital managers, or, in certain circumstances, the patient's nearest relative. The patient himself may seek to obtain his own discharge through a Mental Health Review Tribunal.

Section 5 Change to compulsory detention (applies for 72 hours)

This applies to a patient who is already in hospital on a voluntary basis, but wants and intends to leave. It only requires the recommendation of the doctor in charge or a colleague nominated by him, stating that the patient requires compulsory detention for his own health and safety or that of others. This order should be converted into a Section 2 or 3 as soon as possible.

In an emergency, when a doctor is not available, a registered mental nurse (RMN) or a registered nurse for the mentally impaired may invoke a six-hour holding order. The nurse must record the reasons why the patient needs to be detained compulsorily. The patient must already be in a psychiatric ward or hospital.

Section 136 Mentally disordered person in a public place

Any police constable who finds in a public place someone who appears to be mentally disordered and in need of care and control for his own or others' safety may take him to a 'place of safety'. This is usually a police station or a hospital. The patient can be detained so that he can be examined by a doctor and arrangements made for his care and treatment. The order expires when these arrangements have been made or after 72 hours, whichever is the shorter.

Section 115 Powers of entry and inspection

A social worker, armed with documentation authenticating his status may enter and inspect any premises if there is reason to believe that a mentally disordered person is there and at risk because he is not receiving proper care.

Section 135 Warrant to search for and remove a patient

Any approved social worker who believes that a mentally disordered patient is unable to care for himself, or is being ill-treated, may apply to a magistrate for a warrant for the person's removal to a place of safety.

Social workers may need police back-up in these cases, as ambulance crews are not allowed to transport violent patients.

Section 37 Hospital order

The courts may impose this order, committing an offender to hospital on a similar basis to Section 3, for six months. There must be medical recommendations from two doctors, one of whom must be approved.

Section 41 Restriction order

With a hospital order the court may also apply a restriction order preventing the person's discharge from hospital either for a fixed term or without limit of time. If it is for a fixed term, when that expires the patient will still be detained under a hospital order without restriction: Section 37.

Sections 25A-25J After-care supervision

These sections were inserted into the Mental Health Act by the Mental Health (Patients in the Community) Act 1995. They are aimed at patients, not necessarily offenders, who have been compulsorily detained in hospital, treated and discharged with a care plan, then fail to comply with the plan and deteriorate. They may have repeated relapses and readmissions – the 'revolving door' syndrome – or become involved in anti-social acts. These patients are thought to require 'an especially high degree of supervision' lest they slip through the net of care.

Section 117 After-care

This section applies in general to patients who have previously been detained in hospital under a compulsory order and are discharged. It lays a duty on the Health Authority and the local social services authority to provide after-care services for these patients, normally for as long as they consider these services are needed. In the case of a patient who is subject to 'after-care under supervision' the care must be continued for as long as the supervision order is extant.

When a patient is subject to a supervision order, the Health Authority must ensure:

1   that an approved (Section 12) doctor is in charge of the patient's medical treatment;
2   that someone professionally concerned with one of the after-care services supervises progress to ensure that the patient is receiving proper after-care.

This section was up-dated in 1995 in an attempt to secure better care and control of vulnerable patients, who might become a danger to themselves or to others.

Consent to treatment

In normal circumstances every adult has the right to refuse medical treatment whatever the risk to himself, for instance Jehovah's Witnesses who refuse blood transfusions, or strict Roman Catholic women who may refuse a therapeutic abortion. This is common law. Contentious exceptions are those involving harm to the foetus a woman is carrying: compulsory Caesarean section is a case in point. The common law is legally overridden in the case of patients subject to a treatment order (Sections 3, 2 or 37), and treatment may be imposed on the patient against his wishes. This does not include surgical treatment involving the destruction of brain tissue or its function, and certain other treatments specified by the Secretary of State. Electroconvulsive Therapy (ECT) is not among the latter.

The situation under common law: medical treatment

Two judicial statements may be relevant:

A   Lord Donaldson MR set out this general proposition relating to medical treatment in *Re T (Adult refusal of Medical Treatment)* [1992] 4 All ER 649, 664, CA:

- *Prima facie* every adult has the right and capacity to decide whether or not he will accept medical treatment, even if a refusal may risk permanent injury to his health or even lead to premature death. Furthermore, it matters not whether the reasons for the refusal were rational or irrational, unknown or even non-existent. This is so, notwithstanding the very strong public interest in preserving the life and health of all citizens. However, the capacity of presumption of capacity to decide, which stems from the fact that the patient is an adult, is rebuttable.

- An adult patient may be deprived of his capacity to decide either by long-term mental incapacity or retarded development or by temporary factors such as unconsciousness or confusion or the effects of fatigue, shock, pain or drugs.

- If an adult patient did not have the capacity to decide at the time of the purported refusal and still does not have that capacity, it is the duty of the doctors to treat him in whatever way they consider, in the exercise of their clinical judgment, to be in his best interests.

- Doctors faced with a refusal of consent have to give very careful and detailed consideration to what was the patient's capacity to decide at the time when the decision was made. It may not be a case of capacity or no capacity. It may be a case of reduced capacity. What matters is whether at that time the patient's capacity was reduced below the level needed in the case of a refusal of that importance, for refusals can vary in importance. Some may involve a risk to life or of irreparable damage to health. Others may not.

- In some cases, doctors will not only have to consider the capacity of the patient to refuse treatment, but also whether the refusal has been vitiated because it resulted not only from the patient's will, but from the will of others. It matters not that those others sought, however strongly, to persuade the patient to refuse, so long as in the end the refusal represented the patient's independent decision. If, however, his will was overborne, the refusal will not have represented a true decision. In this context the relationship of the persuader to the patient – for example, spouse, parents or religious adviser – will be important, because some relationships more readily lend themselves to overbearing the patient's will than do others.

- In all cases doctors will need to consider what is the true scope and basis of the refusal. Was it intended to apply in the circumstances which have arisen? Was it based upon assumptions which in the event have not been realised? A refusal is only effective within its true scope and is vitiated if it is based upon false assumptions.

- Forms of refusal should be redesigned to bring the consequences of a refusal forcibly to the attention of patients.

- In cases of doubt as to the effect of a purported refusal of treatment, where failure to treat threatens the patient's life or threatens irreparable damage to his health, doctors and health authorities should not hesitate to apply to the court for assistance.

In the case of *B v Croydon Health Authority* (1994) 22 BMLR 13, a 24 year old detained woman patient suffering from a personality disorder was refusing to eat. The trial judge thought she was capable of a valid refusal, but at appeal Hoffman LJ said he found it hard to accept that 'someone who acknowledges that in refusing food at the critical time she did not appreciate the extent to which she was hazarding her life, was crying out inside for help but unable to break out of the routine of punishing herself, could be said to be capable of making a true choice as to whether to eat'. She was prescribed tube-feeding.

Several cases of anorexia nervosa have been seen in the courts in similar circumstances over recent years. With those who are under 16, however intellectually competent, the ruling is generally in favour of giving treatment.

B. Lord Goff, in the case of *Bolam v Friern Hospital Management Committee* [1957] 2 All ER 118, gave an opinion on the rule that a doctor will be deemed to have acted in the best interests of an incapable patient and will be immune from liability in trespass to the person if he establishes that he acted in accordance with a practice accepted at the time as proper by a responsible body of medical opinion skilled in the particular form of treatment in question. He said that: 'No doubt, in practice, a decision [in the case of serious treatment] may involve others who are concerned with the care of the patient. Sometimes, of course, consultation with a specialist or specialists will be required; and in others, especially where the decision involves more than a purely medical opinion, an interdisciplinary team will in practice participate in the decision. It is very difficult, and would be unwise, for a court to do more that stress that, for those who are involved in these important and sometimes difficult decisions, the overriding consideration is that they should act in the best interests of the person who suffers from the misfortune of being prevented by incapacity from deciding for himself what should be done to his own body in his own best interests.'

What is clear is that in any case of doubt the doctor should involve the whole multidisciplinary team in decision-making in matters that could be controversial, and unless completely satisfied, should apply to the court for guidance.

The *Bolam* principle, so-called, says that: 'a doctor is not guilty of negligence if he has acted in accordance with a practice accepted as proper by a responsible body of medical men skilled in that particular art.' The central issue in *Bolam* was the matter of the information given to the patient and his consent: thought at that time to be necessary to the degree which the profession thought adequate. Nowadays, 40 years later, there is an ever-increasing regard for the patient's autonomy and the acknowledgment that it is his views which dictate what are considered to be appropriate levels of information, not only for research activities but for those which are within the scope of accepted clinical practice.

The Court of Protection

Under certain circumstances the Court of Protection has responsibilities towards the mentally ill or impaired, and these are carried out by the Master and his officers. They, in turn, are advised by medical, legal and general panels of Lord Chancellor's Visitors who visit the patients and review their capacity to manage their own financial and other affairs. Application to the Court of Protection may be made by the nearest relative or any other interested party; he must provide a certificate from the doctor concerned with the patient and an affidavit explaining the patient's property and family. The judge may decide to appoint a receiver, possibly a relative, to manage the patient's affairs under the umbrella of the court.

Using the Court of Protection is only worthwhile if considerable funds are involved since the fees are quite high.

All of these laws and rules apply in England and Wales, and Northern Ireland runs a very similar system. Scotland, however, has always had its individual legal arrangements, and those affecting mental health were reviewed and brought up to date in 1995.

Criminal Procedure (Scotland) Act 1995

This Act came into operation in April 1996. It consolidates and amends various other Acts and provisions and provides new legislation for mentally disordered offenders, particularly in Part VI, Sections 52–63.

Section 52 Committal of accused (untried) defendant to hospital

According to this, an untried defendant who is suffering from a mental disorder may still be committed to hospital as before, but there is now a provision to vary or revoke the committal if there has been a change of circumstances. For example, the patient might require transfer to the state hospital on the one hand if greater security is needed, or on the other, discharge might be appropriate. Committal to hospital may not run for more than 40 days in summary proceedings or 110 days in solemn proceedings.

Sections 54–56 Insanity in bar of trial and at the time of the act

The legal criteria for insanity in bar of trial and at the time of the offence are unchanged, and are laid down in the Mental Health (Scotland) Act 1984, and the Mental Health (Amendment) (Scotland) Act 1983: the court must be satisfied by the evidence of two doctors, at least one of whom must be on the approved list, of the patient's mental status. However, there have been sweeping changes in line with the Thomson Report and the Criminal Procedure (Insanity and Unfitness to Plead) Act 1991 for England and Wales. The major innovations are an examination of the facts in bar of trial and flexible arrangements for disposal in cases of insanity. Insanity at the time of the act or offence is now accepted as a defence.

Defendants who may be insane in bar of trial are subject to a three-stage procedure:

- determining whether or not they are insane in bar of trial;
- examination of the facts of the case;
- decision on disposal.

If the accused person is found insane in bar of trial, the trial must be stopped and the examination of the facts proceed. Meanwhile the defendant may be remanded in custody or committed to hospital under a new temporary order:

Section 54(1)(c)

The examination of facts is very similar to a trial and is usually held in public before a Sheriff or Judge sitting alone, and the accused may be acquitted in the ordinary way. When the defendant is acquitted on grounds of insanity, but is found to have committed the offence, the court may make a hospital order, with or without restrictions, a guardianship order, the new supervision and treatment order, or no order. The exception is in the case of murder, when a hospital order with restrictions on discharge, without limit of time, is mandatory. A supervision and treatment order involves a social worker and a doctor, and runs for a maximum of three years. There is a 'requirement' to submit to treatment under the direction of a doctor but there is no penalty if the offender does not comply.

Section 200 Remand and committal for inquiry into mental condition

The option of detention in hospital for three weeks with the option of a further three weeks is added to remand in prison or on bail for the purpose of a medical examination and report on the person's mental state. To commit an offender to hospital for inquiry into his mental condition requires the written or oral evidence of one doctor. The person may appeal against his committal to hospital within 24 hours.

Section 230 Probation with a requirement for treatment for a mental condition

This now includes treatment under the supervision of a chartered psychologist (the British Psychological Society holds a register) as well as by a doctor. As before, there is a maximum duration of 12 months, an option of residence in a psychiatric hospital, and a requirement for evidence from an approved doctor. The court must be satisfied that proper arrangements for treatment have been made.

BIBLIOGRAPHY

USEFUL SOURCES OF FURTHER READING

Black D, Newman M, Hendriks JH, Mezey G, *Psychological Trauma: a developmental approach*, 1996, London: Gaskell.

Chick J, Cantwell R (eds), *Seminars in Alcohol and Drug Misuse*, 1994, London: Gaskell.

Cicchetti, D, Carlson, V (ed), *Child maltreatment. Theory and Research on the causes and consequences of child abuse and neglect*, 1989, New York: Cambridge University Press.

Cooper JE (ed), *A Pocket Guide to the ICD-10 Classification*, 1994, Edinburgh: Churchill Livingstone.

Diagnostic and Statistical Manual of Mental Disorders, 1994, 4th edn, DSM-IV, Washington: American Psychiatric Association.

Edwards CRW, Bouchier IAD (eds), *Davidson's Principles and Practice of Medicine*, 1991, Edinburgh: Churchill Lingstone.

Faulk M, *Basic Forensic Psychiatry*, 1994, 2nd edn, Oxford: Blackwell.

Gelder M, Gath D, Mayou R, Cowen P, *Oxford Textbook of Psychiatry*, 1996, 3rd edn, Oxford: Oxford University Press.

Gomez J, *Liaison Psychiatry*, 1987, London: Croom Helm.

Guthrie E, Creed F (eds), *Seminars in Liaison Psychiatry*, 1996, London: Gaskell.

ICD-10 Classification of Mental and Behavioural Disorders, 1992, Geneva: World Health Organization.

Jacobson, RR, 'The post-concussional syndrome: physiogenesis, psychogenesis and malingering: an integrative model' (1996) *Journal of Psychosomatic Research* 32, 391–98.

Jones R, *Mental Health Act Manual*, 1996, 5th edn, London: Sweet & Maxwell.

Lishman WA, *Organic Psychiatry*, 1987, 2nd edn, Oxford: Blackwell.

Merskey H, *The Analysis of Hysteria*, 1995, London: Gaskell.

INDEX